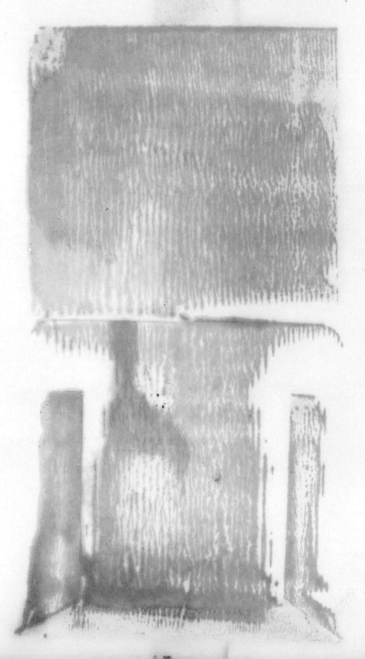

Philosophy
in
Literature

Philosophy

in

Literature

Shakespeare, Voltaire, Tolstoy & Proust

by Morris Weitz
The Ohio State University

Detroit
Wayne State University Press
1963

for Everett Nelson

Contents

Preface

THIS BOOK CONTAINS the text of four lectures given at Wayne State University in April 1961 under the auspices of the English Department. The lectures attempt to show by analyzing four literary masterpieces that philosophy and literature can be combined to their mutual enrichment, not to their mutual impoverishment, as some critics and philosophers maintain. My central problem is to elucidate the aesthetic roles that philosophical ideas play in the literary works that contain them. One reason for my having chosen these particular works is that each of the examples—*Candide, Anna Karenina, Hamlet,* and *A la Recherche du Temps Perdu* —illustrates a different artistic treatment of philosophical ideas. Another reason for my choice is that each of the works invites a fresh interpretation which philosophical analysis can best provide. Each essay, therefore, purports to be a new reading of the particular work analyzed. The essay on *Hamlet* also presents and criticizes certain traditional readings of the play that reduce its philosophy to some aspect of the characterization, dialog, imagery, or plot; thus, in this essay much of the *Hamlet* criticism serves as a paradigm of how philosophy should not be joined with literature.

In addition to the lectures there is an epilog which summarizes the major themes and their implications for literary criticism and aesthetics. I am grateful to Professor Herbert M. Schueller, Chairman of the English Department, and Dr. Harold A. Basilius, Director of the Wayne State University Press, for their suggestion that there be such an epilog. They, as well as Professor Everett J. Nelson, Patricia Davis, editor at the Wayne State University Press, and my wife, read the manuscript; I am grateful to them for their criticisms. I wish also to express my appreciation to my generous audience, to the members of the English Department for their stimulation and hospitality, and to my friends and former teachers at Wayne who gave me the opportunity to repay an old debt. Also, I wish to thank the Guggenheim Foundation for its aid, since the *Hamlet* lecture was prepared during my tenure as a John Simon Guggenheim Memorial Fellow (1959-60).

M. W.

Acknowledgments

Acknowledgments are due to the following for permission to quote:

Penguin Books Ltd. for passages from John Butt's translation of *Candide* by Voltaire.

Random House, Inc. for passages from Constance Garnett's translation of *Anna Karenina* by Leo Tolstoy.

Cambridge University Press for passages from the J. Dover Wilson edition of Shakespeare's *Hamlet*, in *The New Shakespeare*.

Chatto & Windus Ltd. and Random House, Inc. for passages from C. K. Scott Moncrieff and S. Hudson's translation of Marcel Proust's *Remembrance of Things Past*.

I. *Candide:*

THE BURDEN OF PHILOSOPHY

PHILOSOPHY AND LITERATURE have been opposed to each other as often as they have been combined. There is one tradition, stemming from Plato, in which literature is contrasted with philosophy as falsehood is with truth. Another tradition, deriving from Aristotle, has it that, although literature does not constitute a realm of falsehood, it is, at its best, only truth second hand. Better than history, perhaps, literature yet remains lower than philosophy in the hierarchy of man's achievements.

Literary critics have never received kindly this traditional censure of literature. While some have defended literature on moral grounds, other critics have pointed to the limitations inherent in the abstract character of philosophical truth in contrast with the rich, concrete nature of literary truth. Indeed, this quarrel between literature and philosophy is an ancient one. And, as interesting and important as the issues are, it will not be the purpose of these lectures to state, clarify, or resolve the quarrel. Instead, I shall simply pick out one or two of the issues that retain a contemporary interest and importance and test their force in some prime examples of literature. I begin, then, not with Plato's diatribe against literature, but with I. A. Richards' attack on philosophy in literature.

7

Richards' great contribution to the aesthetics of literature was to contend that literature does not consist of truth-claims about the world; it is not philosophy or science. He argued that literature is not a competitor of philosophy and science as a descriptive or an empirical conclusion from semantical premises about the two uses of language, the referential as against the emotive. But it is now quite clear that not only was his semantics woefully inadequate, indeed downright harmful, as its history has shown, but that part of its application, namely, that literature is the emotive use of language, was itself a recommendation that literature ought to be read as such if we were to save it from philosophical or scientific reduction. In effect, then, Richards argued that we should read literature as literature, not as philosophy or anything else.

Richards' conception of literature as emotive and his repudiation of philosophy in literature have had an enormous impact upon recent literary theory and criticism. Of immediate concern to us was his insistence upon the sharp separation between the aims and substances of literature and philosophy. Ironically, his total program has functioned in our thinking about the relation between philosophy and literature as the exact counterpart of Plato's because both agree that the reduction of literature to philosophy or philosophy to literature constitutes a distortion of both.

Although I have no intention of engaging in a full-scale debate with Plato and Richards on their claims about philosophy in relation to literature, I shall question their thesis that literature and philosophy never meet or should never meet in making true claims about the world. But now I wish to examine only their thesis, often accorded the status of dogma in present literary criticism, that literature cannot be joined with philosophy without the distortion and denigration of both.

Literature comprises plays, poems, novels, tales. These are constituted in various ways by characters, dialog, language, theme, plot, and so forth. I skip over the problem whether literature or any of its species or any of its varying constituents can be defined in such a way that sets of necessary or sufficient properties of them can be given. I take it as a philosophical myth, exploded by Wittgenstein, in spite of which the myth retains its power in the ritual pattern of criticism, that nothing can be intelligibly stated about literature or its genres unless we ascertain or at least assume the existence of certain essences that correspond to our genre-terms and guarantee their use. We are absolutely sure that certain works are works of literature, even though we may be unsure of the so-called defining properties of literature. So, too, we can assert all that can be said about drama, poetry, and prose fiction, or about character, dialog, plot, and theme, however ambiguous these are as terms or vague they are as phenomena, without any affirmation or assumption of sets of defining properties of these.

Among the constituents of many literary works are themes or ideas about man, society, and reality. Some of these themes are clearly philosophical in the broad, traditional sense, since they deal with morality, knowledge, human purpose, and reality. In general, these themes or ideas are not stated explicitly in the text; they are exhibited through such structural devices as plot, character, and dialog. Consequently, one task of literary criticism is to elucidate the various ways literature aesthetically assimilates and transmits philosophy. Indeed, my major assignment in these lectures is to try to show, through some examples, how philosophical ideas are embodied in literary works of art which will, by implication, show also that philosophy and literature can be joined.

My model for this elucidation of philosophical themes

in literature is one version of imagistic criticism in contemporary literary criticism. Because it is simply an aesthetic fact that some literary works contain images and because these images are on an aesthetic par with the other elements of literature, one problem for literary criticism is to identify these images and to determine their aesthetic contribution to the whole work of art. In recent literary criticism there have been two important approaches to this problem. The first, represented best by Caroline Spurgeon's studies of Shakespearean drama, consists of the enumeration, abstraction, and classification of the images in the plays. Because Miss Spurgeon feels that imagery is central to each of Shakespeare's dramas, she also feels that the function of the critic is to abstract this imagery from the individual plays, find its dominant tenor, and reduce the meaning of the whole play to this central tenor. Philosophical criticism of literature has often proceeded in a similar abstractive, reductive manner. The critic ferrets out the dominant theme, abstracts it from the context of the whole work, proclaims it central, reduces the whole work to it, and then provides an evaluation of the work in terms of the truth or falsity of this reduction. No wonder that Richards responded to this kind of criticism with his mighty, righteous wrath.

The second imagistic approach is exemplified by W. H. Clemen's studies, also of Shakespearean drama, wherein the emphasis lies on the functional relation and contribution of imagery to the other elements of the individual plays. The imagery is not central, nor is anything else short of the whole work of art. Imagery is but one element in an organically functioning whole. The task, then, of the critic is simply to identify the imagery and to relate it artistically to the other elements of the work.

Therefore, I want to claim for philosophy in literature the same exegetical power that Clemen claims for imagis-

tic analysis. To draw a parallel, it is accepted that literature often contains philosophical themes or ideas, that is,
certain readings of human experience. These ideas are as
aesthetically important as any other elements in the work,
although they are not necessarily central or all important.
Consequently, one job of the literary critic is to ascertain
and to relate these themes or ideas in their artistically
organic context to the other elements, such as, character,
plot, and language. Thus employed as an exegetical tool
of literary criticism, philosophy can be joined effectively
with literature, not in an effort to reduce the work of art
to the philosophical nugget that Richards rightly detested,
but to further and enrich our aesthetic understanding.

It is time now to turn to our first example, *Candide*.
That it is Voltaire's masterpiece everyone, with the exception of the master himself, agrees. That it is successful
as a work of art, that it has met the minimum criterion of
a great work, laid down by Dr. Johnson, namely, "length
of duration and continuance of esteem," and even his
further criterion that "nothing can please many, and
please long, but just representations of general nature,"
can also be claimed without interesting challenge. *Candide* has been read with sheer delight since its anonymous
but scarcely secret publication in Geneva and Paris in
January, 1759. In that year alone, there were some twenty
different editions, mostly piratical ones, and English and
Italian translations as well. When Voltaire died in 1778,
the number of editions of *Candide* had climbed to fifty.
It became the best-seller of the eighteenth century.

Candide has lost none of its eighteenth-century appeal.
Local conditions have changed, but the general butts of
Voltaire's satire have not. Unvictorious English admirals
are no longer shot as object lessons in military persever-
ance, and Jesuits, so far as I know, no longer make good

eating for the worthy descendants of the Oreillons, but there is little diminution in our time of the human scourges of war, famine, rape, avarice, persecution, bigotry, superstition, intolerance, and hypocrisy. For those who hate avoidable human suffering, as Voltaire did, *Candide* still serves as an effectual whip with which to lash once again the perpetuators of this suffering.

But there is a more basic appeal in *Candide* than that provided by the satire, an appeal that inheres in the sheer unfolding of the events themselves and without which the satire would have lost its aesthetic sting long ago. *Candide* is a magnificent romp: satirical, anti-metaphysical, and purely human. It is this human game, comprised of puppet-like characters and their sometimes improbable, often incredible and repetitive adventures, that Voltaire superbly captures through verbal economy, parody, caricature, and episodical vitality. The prose itself is energized by the action. That Voltaire does not allow interest to flag, in spite of the incredibility of character and incident and the reiteration of the theme of human misery, is his primary achievement in integrating philosophy and literature in *Candide*.

"Do you think," asks Candide of Martin as they approach the coast of France, "that men have always massacred each other, as they do today, that they have always been false, cozening, faithless, ungrateful, thieving, weak, inconstant, mean-spirited, envious, greedy, drunken, miserly, ambitious, bloody, slanderous, debauched, fanatic, hypocritical, and stupid?" [1] Martin replies with a further question, "Do you think that hawks have always eaten pigeons when they could find them?" "Of course I do," Candide answers. To this Martin responds, "Well, if hawks have always had the same character, why should you suppose that men have changed theirs?"

Although a survey of the characters in the novel certainly supports much of Martin's assessment—one need think only of the snobbish Baron, the knavish Dutch captain, Vanderdendur, the conniving Brazilian Governor, the bestial Batavian sailor, the hypocritical Jesuits, the avaricious Jews, and the thieving *abbé* from Périgord— it is doubtful that Martin sums up Voltaire's attitude toward humanity. Although Voltaire's gallery of rogues, reproductions of which inhabit the world, is not a flattering series of portraits, it is incorrect to interpret Martin's wholesale condemnation as a true generalization about all the characters. Indeed, Martin and many others are not like the people condemned. The collective misery of human beings may be a fact, but Martin is forced to retract what he says about Cacambo's disloyalty to Candide. Both Martin and Cacambo are loyal, and Jacques the Anabaptist is a kind, charitable Christian. Even Cunégonde's servant, the old woman, possesses commendable moral qualities. Thus, there are people in *Candide* who are neither born nor made wolves, so even Jacques' assessment of humanity does not exhaust the world of the novel. Some of the characters, whatever their shortcomings, are decent, kind, loyal, generous, and sacrificing. Furthermore, there are characters who are more sinned against than sinning, for example, Paquette, Frère Giroflée, and the Negro slave. In addition, there are all the inhabitants of Eldorado, the Turkish farmer, even Pangloss, Cunégonde, and Candide himself, who are far from the evil that Martin claims for all human beings. That all the characters are not immoral constitutes a *donnée* which is of first importance in the formulation and confirmation of any hypothesis about the total philosophy in *Candide*.

It is the plot, more than the characterization or the dialog, which carries the acknowledged major philosophical theme of the novel: that optimism is absurd. How does Voltaire understand optimism in *Candide?* His hero gives the best definition of it: "It's the passion for maintaining that all is right when all goes wrong with us." [2] ("C'est la rage de soutenir que tout est bien quand on est mal.")[3] It is in this sense that Pangloss is an optimist; no matter what the disaster or suffering is, Pangloss insists that it is right. But natural and human evils are not only right; they are also ingredients in the best of all possible worlds—our world—in which all is a pre-established harmony and everything has a good reason for being what it is.

Now, Pangloss may be incredible but he is consistent, never once forsaking his passion for maintaining that all is right, for the best, and cosmically rational, whether the suffering is his or someone else's. His optimism may be harmless, as it is when he explains why we have noses, so we can carry spectacles; it may be callous, as it is when he justifies the drowning of Jacques in the harbor of Lisbon or the effects of the earthquake on the inhabitants of Lisbon; it may be frightful, as it is when he extols the maximization of private misfortunes on the grounds that it increases the total amount of good in the world; it may be fantastic, as it is when he justifies the ravages of syphilis in him and others because it has also brought Europe chocolate and cochineal; it may be obtuse, as it is when he persists that all is for the best, in spite of his abortive hanging, painful dissection, and brutal enslavement; it may even be flexible, as it is when he concedes to the Turkish farmer and to Candide that man was made to work in this best of all possible worlds; but it is consistent. Ultimately, optimism is as self-accommodating and self-protecting an hypothesis about the world as one could imagine or hope for, since absolutely nothing can refute it. Remember Pangloss' final words:

"There is a chain of events in this best of all possible worlds; for if you had not been turned out of a beautiful mansion at the point of a jackboot for the love of Lady Cunégonde, and if you had not been involved in the Inquisition, and had not wandered over America on foot, and had not struck the Baron with your sword, and lost all those sheep you brought from Eldorado, you would not be here eating candied fruit and pistachio nuts." [4]

Optimism, then, as Voltaire interprets it, does not deny the existence of natural disasters or human suffering; it denies only that these phenomena are evil, asserting instead that they are necessary features of a world than which none can be better.

It is sometimes said and often implied that Voltaire's interpretation is a caricature of the optimistic philosophies prevalent in his day, especially those of Leibniz and Pope. Although the Panglossian version may distort somewhat the philosophies of Leibniz or Pope, it does not distort their theories of evil. For however they differ from Pangloss or from each other on the metaphysical trimmings, all three doctrines concur that all is right when all is wrong, that recognized natural and human evils are aspects of the good, and that this is the best of all possible worlds. If optimism is construed as the view that evil is really good, then Pangloss speaks consummatively not only for Leibniz and Pope, but also for many other philosophers, even as far back as Plato who in the *Timaeus* formulates for the first time the doctrine that all imperfection is a necessary ingredient of total perfection. Pangloss speaks also for all people—philosophers or not—who believe in the existence of a Supreme Being, that is, a God who is all-powerful, all-knowing, and all-good. For it is logically impossible to affirm the existence of such a Being and at the same time to deny that all is right, that this is the best of all possible worlds, and that natural and human evils are really good. Whether Voltaire knew it or not, or whether he wished it or not, he was playing for keeps in *Candide*.

How, now, does Voltaire show that optimism is absurd? As I have suggested, he does it mostly through the plot. *Candide* is a series of natural and human disasters; human beings suffer through war, rape, famine, drowning, earthquake, debauchery, violence, torture, brutality, indifference, intolerance, deception, persecution, slavery, butchery, and disease. No one escapes, except the inhabitants of Eldorado. Individuals even outdo each other in the disclosure of their woes. Happiness is but a superficial smile or moment of experience which dissolves upon questioning or in the next moment. Much of this human misery seems avoidable, although, to be sure, some of it, like some of the effects of the natural evils of storms and earthquakes, is not. Voltaire piles up relentlessly, one on top of the other, these human miseries. As fantastic and incredible as the accumulation is, the individual miseries are not, and we are led inevitably to the conclusion that all is not right when all goes wrong, that this cannot be the best of all possible worlds—it may even be the worst, as Martin seems to suggest—and that evil cannot be assimilated by good. Indeed, we are led to the further conclusion at the end of the novel that perhaps the worst evil of all is the promotion of the optimistic philosophy. It is this philosophy which is the burden that man must throw off if he is to make life tolerable.

Voltaire does not attempt to refute optimism by argument. Rather he reduces it to absurdity by his narration of human life as a series of disasters. Of course, his narration is not a formal refutation or *reductio ad absurdum* of optimism; he calls into question no ultimate premise of optimism, nor does he point out the vacuously irrefutable character of the optimistic hypothesis about the world. His is the dramatic technique of showing the absurdity of the doctrine. And in showing that optimism is absurd, Voltaire meets, once more, successfully, the burden of philosophy, this time the artistic problem of getting a philosophical idea or, if one like, a counter-philosophical idea into literature.

Optimism functions as a counsel of despair, not of joy or hope. It cannot explain, as it was intended to, the existence of evil. Evil simply exists and it is man's task to cope with it as best he can, not to speculate on its ultimate *raison d'être*. To alleviate those evils that Voltaire thinks are contingent and avoidable, man must substitute useful labor for optimism or idle speculation on the philosophical problem of evil. "Work," says the Turkish farmer to Candide, Martin, and Pangloss, "banishes those three great evils, boredom, vice, and poverty." [5] Pangloss concedes this, once he rationalizes work as part of the necessary, benevolent scheme of things. Martin says, "We must work without arguing, that is the only way to make life bearable." And Candide concludes, "We must go and work in the garden." [6] (". . . Il faut cultiver notre jardin.") [7]

The significance of this collective substitution of honest labor for idle speculation is that it is better to work than to philosophize about insoluble problems. But even though honest labor is better than idle argument, it cannot eliminate evil. If the Turkish farmer be right, work can eliminate one set of evils: boredom, vice, and poverty. But, unless everyone were to accept the recommendation, it does not mitigate other evils, for example, war. Even the Turkish farmer is too intelligent not to see that what happens to hundreds of his countrymen every day in Constantinople can also happen to him tomorrow. Hence, Candide's injunction that "We must cultivate the garden" cannot seriously imply that each of us, singly or collectively, is to turn his back on the world and wall up his little hothouse, perhaps as Epicurus and his friends did. Our guarantee against human rapacity would be no greater under these circumstances than that of the smug coterie at Thunder-ten-tronckh.

Voltaire must mean something other than to enclose oneself in an injunction to work. One possible interpretation that suggests itself is to generalize or universalize the recommendation; it is necessary for everyone to cultivate the garden. In this interpretation, work approximates justice in Plato's *Republic* in that each of us is to do what he can do best with the result that each helps himself as well as his brother. Cunégonde becomes an excellent pastry cook, Paquette learns to embroider, the old woman takes to laundering, Giroflée becomes a good carpenter, and Candide, Martin, and even Pangloss discover and work at what they can do best. On this scheme, there exists an honest job for each of us which, when persevered in, leaves no time for either idle talk or small- or large-scale prosecution of vice and evil. The garden now encompasses the world; its inhabitants cultivate it in the Platonic sense wherein each does what he can do best. The formula operates in Eldorado—a world all its own—so why cannot this formula be applied in the rest of the globe?

Does Voltaire conclude *Candide* with this utopian vision of the resolution of all avoidable human evils? Can the cultivation of the garden of the world bring man happiness? Work in its Platonic sense can cure all the avoidable evils of human life, provided, of course, that man first relinquish optimism for the fraud it is. But work cannot bring real happiness, nor can anything else. And this claim can be substantiated by turning to what can only be referred to as the neglected theme of *Candide*.

The common critical interpretation of Eldorado is that

it represents the blissful life of peace, prosperity, kindness, personal honesty, religious tolerance, intellectual integrity, and sweet reasonableness. It serves as a perpetual reminder of the desirable and the unattainable; and, as such, it also functions dramatically in *Candide* as a foil to the real world. Consequently, Eldorado is the ideal world of virtue and happiness in contrast to the real world of vice and misery. It is a utopian existence because it is beyond the reach of ordinary human beings.

However, Eldorado was not beyond the reach of Candide and Cacambo, for they were there. But, it was certainly not their choice or preference; they chose to leave Eldorado for the world outside because:

> They spent a month at the palace, but not a day passed without Candide saying to Cacambo: "It is quite true, my good fellow, that the house where I was born won't bear comparison with the mansions of this country; but still, I shall never be happy without Lady Cunégonde, and I dare say you have some mistress or other in Europe. If we stay here, we shall be no different from anybody else; but if we go back to the old world with a mere twelve sheep laden with Eldorado stones, we shall be richer than all the Kings of Europe put together." [8]

Voltaire continues (and here I quote the French, because the exact wording is important):

> Ce discours plut à Cacambo: on aime tant à courir, à se faire valoir chez les siens, à faire parade de ce qu'on a vu dans ses voyages, que les deux heureux résolurent de ne plus l'être et de demander leur congé à Sa Majesté. [9]

Translations differ here. One reads:

> Cacambo was pleased at this, for, like Candide, he had a restless spirit. They were both anxious, also, to show their friends how rich they had grown and to boast about what they had seen in their travels. So these

happy men decided to be happy no longer and to take leave of His Majesty.[10]

Another translates *"on aime tant à courir"* as "it is so pleasant to be on the move," [11] and my French friends say the phrase also means and probably meant to Voltaire "one loves to chase skirts." Whatever the exact meaning, the spirit of this passage is unmistakable. Candide and Cacambo want to leave their utopia because they want something else. They are restless; and consequently, they are human. They choose not to remain happy.

Regardless of the role of utopias in eighteenth-century fiction, Eldorado in *Candide* is not an unrealizable ideal for man, but a realized ideal that is rejected. The decision of Candide and Cacambo to return to the real world betokens the neglected theme of the novel—that man does not want utopian happiness. The old woman is the first to articulate this theme, after recounting her trials and tribulations:

> "I have wanted to kill myself a hundred times, but somehow I am still in love with life. This ridiculous weakness is perhaps one of our most melancholy propensities; for is there anything more stupid than to be eager to go on carrying a burden which one would gladly throw away, to loathe one's very being and yet to hold it fast, to fondle the snake that devours us until it has eaten our hearts away?" [12]

She expands on this idea toward the close of the novel, when the little group is reunited in Constantinople:

> "I should like to know which is the worst, to be ravished a hundred times by negro pirates, to have one buttock cut off, to run the gauntlet of a Bulgar regiment, to be whipped and hanged at an auto-da-fé, to be dissected, to row in the galleys—in fact, to experience all the miseries through which we have passed— or just to stay here with nothing to do?" [13]

But it is Martin who sums it up in one of his few non-Manichean moments:

> Martin's conclusion was that man was born to suffer from the restlessness of anxiety or from the lethargy of boredom.[14]
> (. . . Martin surtout conclut que l'homme était né pour vivre dans les convulsions de l'inquiétude, ou dans la léthargie de l'ennui.)[15]

Many incidents in the novel, and especially the crucial rejection of Eldorado by Candide and Cacambo, dramatize Martin's philosophical summation of human experience. Man is presented as essentially a bipolar creature, oscillating between his restlessness of anxiety and his lethargy of boredom. He may dream of the eradication of avoidable evils and of a utopian bliss; he may even accept the goal of work without rebelling. But basically he wants what he has—his oscillation—with all its attendant variety. He loves life—the romp itself—even more than he desires either the obliteration of evils or the happy boredom of utopia. With this theme we reach the third and final burden of philosophy in *Candide,* Voltaire's own insight into the human condition which, because more artist than *philosophe*, he was able successfully to translate dramatically into his novel.

II. *Anna Karenina:*

PHILOSOPHY AND THE WORD

THERE IS LITTLE PHILOSOPHY on the printed pages of *Anna Karenina*, because Tolstoy generally forgoes commenting on or interpreting the characters he delineates, their dialog, and the events of their lives. His technique throughout is that of direct narration or description of character and event. When necessary, he does provide the reader with relevant background material before the action of the novel begins. But apart from a few observations on extremely obvious human traits, such as, the tendency to forget our troubles by living in the needs of the day or the natural ability of children to distinguish between genuine and feigned affection, Tolstoy does not comment on the material he presents and describes.

However, commentary is provided in part by the characters themselves, through bits of dialog and soliloquy that are philosophical, for example, the conversation on philosophical materialism between Levin's half-brother, Sergey Koznishev, and an important but unnamed professor from Harkov. But Levin's impatience with the superficiality of the debate and his uninvited question, brushed aside by the irritated professor, reduce this particular philosophical discussion to a triviality. But, although important, such issues as the role of aristocratic values in society, Levin's relationship to God, and the examination of blame and judgment can not be pulled out of their dramatic contexts in order to be interpreted as philosophically central in the novel. If *Anna Karenina* be a philosophical novel, or even if there be an important philosophical theme that relates and contributes to the whole work, one must go beneath the dialog, soliloquy, and sparse commentary to discover it.

In the same sense that the human romp determines and harmonizes with the philosophy of *Candide*, the pervasive tone of *Anna Karenina* is its largess, the sympathetic presentation of the abundance of nature and human life. Whatever is said philosophically and aesthetically about *Anna Karenina* must derive from and return to this abundance which is the tonic of the whole composition. Eating, dancing, racing, hunting, farming, marrying, even partying occupy much of the novel. Tolstoy lingers over each of these activities as he conveys its full, qualitative richness. Recollect some of the eating episodes of the novel. Two are arranged and presided over by the tasteful, master Cyrenaic, Stepan Oblonsky, and another is the meal before the hunt at Levin's country home where, once again, Oblonsky is present. An early chapter presents with great care and flavor a delectable meal consisting of oysters, soup, turbot, roast beef, capons, cheese, and Chablis. Even Levin's truculence, caused by his disdain for the decadent restaurant and food and by his anxiety over Kitty, does not spoil the delights of the menu. And Oblonsky's later marketing expedition on behalf of his propitious dinner party at which Kitty and Levin are reunited is also related with an author's pride that Proust himself might have envied as he sent Françoise through half the markets of Paris to ensure the success of the dinner party for M. de Norpois.

Or consider the fateful ball. Tolstoy narrates more than the conflict between Kitty and Anna over Vronsky; he paints the whole glittering scene with a womanly respect for detail that certainly suggests sympathy for all the pleasures of the ball. His description of Kitty entering the ballroom is almost motherly:

> It was one of Kitty's best days. Her dress was not uncomfortable anywhere; her lace berthe did not droop anywhere; her rosettes were not crushed nor torn off; her pink slippers with high, hollowed-out heels did not pinch, but gladdened her feet; and the thick rolls of fair chignon kept up on her head as if they were her own hair. All the three buttons buttoned up without tearing on the long glove that covered her hand without concealing its lines. The black velvet of her locket nestled with special softness round her neck. That velvet was delicious; at home, looking at her neck in the looking-glass, Kitty had felt that that velvet was speaking. About all the rest there might be a doubt, but the velvet was delicious.[1]

How superbly tender this description is. How dramatic it becomes when it is compared with the famous portrayal of Anna in her black velvet gown that Kitty had expected and wished to be lilac. The dancing starts, Vronsky capitulates to Anna, and Kitty's delicious velvet is figuratively torn to shreds. Tolstoy here performs an artistic miracle in bringing together this opulence of dress, decor, and drama.

Once more Tolstoy creates a scene full of mass excitement in the race in which Vronsky ineptly breaks the back of his beloved Frou-Frou. The excitement, of course, reaches its climax in Vronsky's fall, followed by Anna's anguish which is so painfully visible to her husband, and culminates in Anna's confession to her husband that she is Vronsky's mistress. Nevertheless, much of the pageantry surrounding the actual race and the resultant incidents is surveyed and lingered upon simply for its own sake as a perennial source of human gratification.

Hunting also is one of life's pleasures, as even this single paragraph shows:

> Levin looked about him to right and to left, and there, just facing him against the dusky blue sky above the confused mass of tender shoots of the aspens, he saw the flying bird. It was flying straight towards him; the guttural cry, like the even tearing of some strong stuff, sounded close to his ear; the long beak and neck of the bird could be seen, and at the very instant when Levin was taking aim, behind the bush where Oblonsky stood, there was a flash of red lightning: the bird dropped like an arrow, and darted upwards again. Again came the red flash and the sound of a blow, and fluttering its wings as though trying to keep up in the air, the bird halted, stopped still an instant, and fell with a heavy splash on the slushy ground.[2]

Farming is also extolled. Indeed, here Levin is in his element, whether he is attending his prize calves, his unworkable machines, his recalcitrant peasants, or his beloved fields. Tolstoy's descriptions of these activities become positively ecstatic at times, especially the one of Levin's mowing. Tolstoy sees in man's working in and through nature a kind of fulness of being that represents what nature has wrought to achieve one sort of human perfection:

> The longer Levin mowed, the oftener he felt the moments of unconsciousness in which it seemed not his hands that swung the scythe, but the scythe mowing of itself, a body full of life and consciousness of its own, and as though by magic, without thinking of it, the work turned out regular and well-finished of itself. These were the most blissful moments.[3]

Finally, let us look at the wedding of Kitty and Levin —replete with all the ever-appealing details of the crowd inside and outside the church, the attendants, the bride and groom, the anxieties, the ceremony, the candles, the rings, and the women's tears over their own marriages— which is a majestic rendition of one of the great moments of human life. The whole tone of the description, matched by the richness of the experience described, sounds in harmony with the lofty choir in the church itself. Similarly, Tolstoy depicts courtship, birth, death, and conversion with the same qualitative richness that the experiences themselves contain.

On the other hand, some activities are treated in a distinctly different tone. Sarcastic touches appear in the depictions of opera- and theatergoing, political meetings, and afterdinner parties. One example of this change in tone will suffice:

> Round the samovar and the hostess the conversation had been meanwhile vacillating in just the same way between three inevitable topics: the latest piece of public news, the theater, and scandal. It, too, came finally to rest on the last topic, that is, ill-natured gossip.[4]

Tolstoy arouses the greatest surprise by his absolute silence on the fundamental human activity of sex. He does not dwell upon sex in an attempt to evoke its rich sensuality or to establish its rightful place in the economy of human values, but chooses instead to single out its potentially horrible aftermath by comparing adultery to murder. Vronsky has just seduced Anna after pursuing her for a year:

> She felt so sinful, so guilty, that nothing was left her but to humiliate herself and beg forgiveness; and as now there was no one in her life but him, to him she addressed her prayer for forgiveness. Looking at him, she had a physical sense of her humiliation, and she could say nothing more. He felt what a murderer must feel, when he sees the body he has robbed of life. That

body, robbed by him of life, was their love, the first stage of their love. There was something awful and revolting in the memory of what had been bought at this fearful price of shame. Shame at their spiritual nakedness crushed her and infected him. But in spite of all the murderer's horror before the body of his victim, he must hack it to pieces, hide the body, must use what he has gained by his murder.

And with fury, as it were with passion, the murderer falls on the body, and drags it and hacks at it; so he covered her face and shoulders with kisses.[5]

Tolstoy sees this sexual act as Vronsky and Anna see it, as an act of shame. Although critical of the immoral society women who castigate and ostracize Anna, the frigidity of Alexey Karenin, and the uncharitable religiosity of Countess Lidia Ivanovna, there is nothing else in the whole novel that approaches the intensity of the naked shame that Tolstoy shares with Anna in her seduction. No correct statement of the philosophy of *Anna Karenina* can neglect this shame. It indicates that, although life, as Tolstoy perceives it, is good in its rich variety of satisfying experiences and although the sensual plays a rightful and full role in our lives, Anna's adultery can have no place in human abundance because it does not create; it destroys.

But the shame, humiliation, and guilt which epitomize Anna after the seduction scene are abandoned for an admiration and sympathy which are shown no one else in the novel. Her stature as a human being—her beauty, grace, kindness, love, honesty, integrity, and suffering—is unequaled. In a crucial passage Anna reacts to a letter from her husband requesting her to break with Vronsky and return to Petersburg:

"He's right! . . . of course, he's always right; he's a Christian, he's generous! Yes, vile, base creature! And no one understands it except me, and no one ever will;

and I can't explain it. They say he's so religious, so high-principled, so upright, so clever; but they don't see what I've seen. They don't know how he has crushed my life for eight years, crushed everything that was living in me—he has not once even thought that I'm a live woman who must have love. They don't know how at every step he's humiliated me, and been just as pleased with himself. Haven't I striven, striven with all my strength, to find something to give meaning to my life? Haven't I struggled to love him, to love my son when I could not love my husband? But the time came when I knew that I couldn't cheat myself any longer, that I was alive, that I was not to blame, that God has made me so that I must love and live . . ." [6]

Anna, a beautiful, affectionate young girl, is married off by an aunt to an older man who ". . . every time he had stumbled against life itself he had shrunk away from it." [7] She meets Vronsky, who falls madly in love with her; she resists until she can fight no longer; she experiences shame and humiliation; but then she comes alive ". . . like a hungry man who has been given food." [8] But although Anna commits adultery, it is not clearly established that her act, its motivation, and its consequences were immoral or, on the other hand, that they were moral and part of her own salvation or self-realization, perhaps even legitimate processes in the true abundance of human life. After all, the alternative to adultery would have been further suffocation.

Furthermore, upon examining the other characters' attitudes and reactions to Anna, it is evident that those characters who hate her, with the exception of Kitty, are those characters whom Tolstoy detests: Vronsky's mother, Countess Lidia, and Madame Kartasov. Alexey Karenin's hate is too complicated for our present formula, but it is true that Tolstoy respects him only in the forgiveness scene with Vronsky when Anna is dying.

Now, consider the stature of those who love or come

to admire Anna. After discounting her brother and her lover, this still leaves many admirers, including Dolly and late in the novel (shall I say conclusively?) Levin. Here is Dolly on her way to see Anna:

"And they attack Anna. What for? am I any better? I have, anyway, a husband I love—not as I should like to love him, still I do love him, while Anna never loved hers. How is she to blame? She wants to live. God has put that in our hearts. Very likely I should have done the same. Even to this day I don't feel sure I did right in listening to her at that terrible time when she came to me in Moscow. I ought then to have cast off my husband and have begun my life fresh. I might have loved and have been loved in reality. And is it any better as it is?" [9]

And here is Levin's similarly sympathetic reaction to Anna after his first, long-prepared-for meeting with her:

And Levin saw a new trait in this woman, who attracted him so extraordinarily. Besides wit, grace, and beauty, she had truth. [Perhaps 'truthfulness' or 'sincerity' is a better translation of *pravdivost'* than 'truth.'] She had no wish to hide from him all the bitterness of her position. As she said that she sighed, and her face suddenly taking a hard expression, looked as it were turned to stone. With that expression on her face she was more beautiful than ever; but the expression was new; it was utterly unlike that expression, radiant with happiness and creating happiness, which had been caught by the painter in her portrait. Levin looked more than once at the portrait and at her figure, as taking her brother's arm she walked with him to the high doors and he felt for her a tenderness and pity at which he wondered himself. [10]

Immediately after this scene in which Levin, the epitome of moral virtue in the novel, accepts Anna completely, tenderly, and perhaps even lovingly, Oblonsky admonishes him not to be so hard on people in the future. Oblonsky's is not a casual request. Indeed, it is the dramatic culmination of one persistent theme that runs through the dialog from the beginning to the end. Because human beings are not to blame for what they do, it is not for any of us to judge them. The presence of this theme must be acknowledged in any adequate philosophical reading of the novel. Oblonsky first states this theme in the opening chapter as he reflects upon the quarrel between him and his wife over his recently discovered infidelity:

> "Yes, she won't forgive me, and she can't forgive me. And the most awful thing about it is that it's all my fault—all my fault, though I'm not to blame. That's the point of the whole situation . . ." [11]

He varies this idea somewhat in the restaurant when he defends his behavior against Levin's attack:

> "You have a character that's all of a piece, and you want the whole of life to be of a piece too—but that's not how it is . . . You want a man's work, too, always to have a defined aim, and love and family life always to be undivided—and that's not how it is. All the variety, all the charm, all the beauty of life is made up of light and shadow." [12]

Levin states the theme next as he reflects upon his brother Nikolay's life:

> Levin felt that, in spite of all the ugliness of his life, his brother Nikolay, in his soul, in the very depths of his soul, was no more in the wrong than the people who despised him. He was not to blame for having been born with his unbridled temperament and his somehow limited intelligence. [13]

Vronsky reiterates it when Anna reproaches him for following her back to Petersburg:

"What am I coming for?" he repeated, looking straight into her eyes. "You know that I have come to be where you are," he said; "I can't help it." [14]

Anna also echoes the theme when she says to Karenin:

". . . I'm a guilty woman, I'm a bad woman, but I am the same as I was, as I told you then, and I have come to tell you that I can change nothing";[15]

and asserts the same to Dolly:

"But I was not to blame. And who is to blame? What's the meaning of being to blame? Could it have been otherwise?" [16]

After she explains to Dolly that she cannot ask Karenin for a divorce because it would mean giving up her son forever, she states:

"It is only those two creatures [Seryozha, her son, and Vronsky] that I love, and one excludes the other. I can't have them together, and that's the only thing I want. And since I can't have that, I don't care about the rest. I don't care about anything, anything. And it will end one way or another, and so I can't, I don't like to talk of it. So don't blame me, don't judge me for anything. You can't with your pure heart understand all that I'm suffering";[17]

and finally, her last words to Levin who has just accepted her completely:

"Tell your wife that I love her as before, and that if she cannot pardon me my position, then my wish for her is that she may never pardon it. To pardon it, one must go through what I have gone through, and may God spare her that." [18]

My last example is from the end of the novel. Anna is dead; Vronsky has enlisted in the war against the Turks; Vronsky's none-too-savory mother is seeing him off. Speaking to Levin's half-brother, Sergey, she finishes her calumny of Anna:

"Yes, hers was the fitting end for such a woman. Even the death she chose was low and vulgar."

To which Sergey replies:

"It's not for us to judge, countess." [19]

Is this persistent theme that human beings are not to blame for their actions and hence should not judge one another the clue to the philosophy of the novel? How does it relate to the other *données* that much of human life is good and that Anna's adultery is not?

As intriguing as the view may be that responsibility and hence moral judgment are inapplicable to fundamental human decisions and actions because these are determined by instinctual needs and desires as well as by crucial events over which we have no control, it cannot be identified as the main philosophical theme in the novel. For, if it is, the philosophy of *Anna Karenina* constitutes a denial of morality altogether, which clearly conflicts with much of the novel, especially Anna's shame and self-destruction. Furthermore, to accept this theme as central necessitates its application to all experience, not only Anna's affair, but all the hypocrisy, frigidity, and vacuity which are actually deplored in the novel. Finally, such a reading of the novel demands that Oblonsky become its true spokesman, forever pleading for the attitude of laissez faire in human life, and thus reduces the novel to a moral mockery. Consequently, in spite of the presence of this theme in the dialog, Tolstoy's novel in its totality cannot be conceived of as an expression of the philosophy that anything goes, or even that human life is too complex to be comprehended or judged by any single formula about what is right and wrong, good and bad.

Therefore, Anna cannot be interpreted as the apotheosis of self-realization, nor can her suicide be glorified as the tragic finale of a human being who goes down in heroic defeat at the hands of a cruel, morally-infested society. There is, then, an unresolved ambivalence toward Anna in the novel. She is presented as immoral in her adultery and yet moral in her deepest feelings. Is Anna's whole life an intrinsic part of human abundance or is it a violation of it? This question crystallizes the central philosophical question of the novel. And the answer is to be found in the epigraph of the novel, taken from Paul in Rom. 12:19, which relates to and reinforces the whole of the novel:

> Dearly beloved, avenge not yourselves, but rather give place unto wrath: for it is written, Vengeance is mine; I will repay, saith the Lord.

Because vengeance is God's prerogative and because it is man's duty to understand and love, to give and forgive, the Word of God has become the flesh of *Anna Karenina*. Human beings *are* morally responsible for their basic decisions and actions; but, when these are wrong, it is not for any of us to blame or judge, only to understand and forgive; God will do the rest. Ironically enough, it is Anna who first states this theme of forgiveness when she tries to reconcile Dolly and the errant Oblonsky. Dolly asks if Anna could forgive infidelity, and Anna replies:

> "I don't know, I can't judge. . . . Yes, I can. . . . Yes, I could forgive it. I could not be the same, no; but I could forgive it, and forgive it as though it had never been, never been at all. . . ."

To which Dolly gratefully answers:

"Oh, of course, . . . else it would not be forgiveness. If one forgives, it must be completely, completely." [20]

But it is Alexey Karenin who speaks eloquently for forgiveness in his greatest scene which is one of the superb moments of the whole novel. Anna is dying from the aftereffects of the birth of her child by Vronsky. Both Vronsky and the reluctant Karenin are present. On the third day of Anna's agony, Vronsky, alone with Karenin, begs to be spared. Karenin replies, taking Vronsky by the hand:

> "I beg you to hear me out; it is necessary. I must explain my feelings, the feelings that have guided me and will guide me, so that you may not be in error regarding me. You know I had resolved on a divorce, and had even begun to take proceedings. I won't conceal from you that in beginning this I was in uncertainty, I was in misery; I will confess that I was pursued by a desire to revenge myself on you and on her. When I got the telegram, I came here with the same feelings; I will say more, I longed for her death. But . . ." He paused, pondering whether to disclose or not to disclose his feeling to him. "But I saw her and forgave her. And the happiness of forgiveness has revealed to me my duty. I forgive completely. I would offer the other cheek, I would give my cloak if my coat be taken. I pray to God only not to take from me the bliss of forgiveness!"
>
> Tears stood in his eyes, and the luminous, serene look in them impressed Vronsky.
>
> "This is my position: you can trample me in the mud, make me the laughing-stock of the world, I will not abandon her, and I will never utter a word of reproach to you. . . . My duty is clearly marked for me; I ought to be with her, and I will be. . . ."

Tolstoy concludes this scene:

> He [Vronsky] did not understand Alexey Alexandrovitch's feeling, but he felt that it was something higher and even unattainable for him with his view of life.[21]

37

Forgiveness leads to compassion, man's highest virtue. Dolly has it, Varenka has it, Levin has it, even Kitty achieves it. Karenin has it, but only for a moment, for soon his compassion dissolves into self-pity, emotional numbness, and, finally, religious charlatanism.

Interwoven with this plea for compassion is the other thematic statement that "Vengeance is mine; I will repay." This idea is conveyed primarily through the plot and especially through the events which concern the relations between the men and women, the husbands and wives. One way to look at *Anna Karenina* is as a novel about four families, or maybe five if the Vronsky-Anna relationship is included. (It is interesting to note, though not important for my immediate purpose, that one early draft of *Anna Karenina* was called *Two Marriages*, another *Two Couples*.) Each family's story is presented and interrelated by Tolstoy who, like a great composer, states, varies, and harmonizes his themes in creating a "Domestic Symphony." The Shtcherbatskys, the Oblonskys, the Levins, the Karenins, and the Vronskys provide Tolstoy with sufficient material to run through the gamut of family happenings and activities. In the main, these activities emphasize and reinforce the pervasive largess of human life. In spite of the boredom, deception, and humiliation which are inherent in family life so honestly depicted by Tolstoy, the family is nevertheless represented as the center of much that is creative. It is also suggested but not stressed that the family is sacred or inviolable. However, the Anna-Vronsky combination remains the one dissonance in the entire symphony, because there is something in it that violates the very principle of largess, which is the principle of creativity. Anna desperately pursues this principle, but in the end can only destroy it, first in herself, then in Vronsky. Her suicide is the inevitable consummation of her violation of nature's requirement that we create because without creativity the human abundance she sought is impossible.

Thus, Anna is responsible for her adultery, but her punishment is not for this act alone—after all, Oblonsky prospers in his infidelity. In addition, she is punished for her refusal to give Vronsky more children, preferring to keep her beauty and hence, she thinks, his love, and for her emasculation of Vronsky's independence, provoked by her ever-increasing jealousy. In effect, her great sin is this double abortion of herself and her relationship with Vronsky, induced by the shame and humiliation of her first act of adultery which prevented her from requesting of her husband the kind of divorce she wished. The ways of God are devious indeed. And part of what Tolstoy does in *Anna Karenina* is to show stunningly just how God wreaks His vengeance on Anna, by letting her do it for Him. As a woman, defined by nature as an agent of creation, she commits herself to a path that can lead only to destruction for her, her love, and her lover. Unlike Kitty, or the Princess Shtcherbatsky, or even the long-suffering, humiliated Dolly, Anna cannot bring to fruition a relationship that is predisposed to destruction. In the end, Tolstoy's ambivalence toward Anna is not resolved, but merely recast. Anna is justly punished for her transgression against the (perhaps) divine but certainly natural principle of creativity without which there is no good in human life. As artist Tolstoy can, like God, lay out the punishment; but, because he is also human, he refrains from judgment, offering in its place the forgiveness and compassion so highly valued. It is, he shows, our duty to understand, love, and forgive Anna. God has already done the rest.

III. *Hamlet:*

PHILOSOPHY THE INTRUDER

T. S. ELIOT, in his essay "Hamlet," remarks,
". . . Hamlet the character has had an especial temptation for that most dangerous type of critic: the critic with a mind which is naturally of the creative order, but which through some weakness in creative power exercises itself in criticism instead." [1] However true Eliot's insight may be, there exists an even greater temptation for an even more dangerous type of critic and that is the temptation to concentrate upon the philosophical meaning of the play or hero for that kind of critic with a mind which is naturally of the philosophical order, but which through some weakness in philosophical power and, it must be added, aesthetic power, exercises itself in philosophical criticism instead. For the great scandal of *Hamlet* criticism has not been in the reduction of the play to the character of Hamlet, as Eliot suggests, but in the reduction of the play to some one philosophical theme that is abstracted from either the character of Hamlet, the soliloquies, the dialog, the plot, the imagery, or the general atmosphere of the play and is then proclaimed the meaning of the play.

The soliloquies and dialog especially, from Polonius' precepts of worldy wisdom to Hamlet's meditations on life and death, seem to cry out for philosophical generalization. *Hamlet* abounds in ostensibly key passages, for example:

> HAMLET: So, oft it chances in particular men,
> That for some vicious mole of nature in them,
> As in their birth, wherein they are not guilty
> (Since nature cannot choose his origin),
> By the o'ergrowth of some complexion,
> Oft breaking down the pales and forts of reason,
> Or by some habit, that too much o'er-leavens
> The form of plausive manners—that these men,
> Carrying I say the stamp of one defect,
> Being nature's livery, or fortune's star,
> His virtues else be they as pure as grace,
> As infinite as man may undergo,
> Shall in the general censure take corruption
> From that particular fault: the dram of evil
> Doth all the noble substance of a doubt,
> To his own scandal.
>
> (I, 4, 23-38)[2]

This passage and the statement that we are about to see the tragedy of a man who could not make up his mind become the opening lines of the Prolog to Sir Laurence Olivier's film version of *Hamlet*. But this passage, both before and after the appearance of the film, has been accepted widely by many critics of *Hamlet* as the meaning of the entire drama because it reflects an instance of the Aristotelian concept of *hamartia* or tragic flaw.

A second example of philosophical dialog is:

HAMLET: Denmark's a prison.
ROSENCRANTZ: Then is the world one.
HAMLET: A goodly one, in which there are many confines, wards and dungeons; Denmark being one o' th' worst.
ROSENCRANTZ: We think not so, my lord.
HAMLET: Why, then 'tis none to you; for there is noth-

ing either good or bad, but thinking makes it so: to me it is a prison.

(II, 2, 246-254)

How nicely this exchange, especially Hamlet's expression of moral subjectivism, invites generalization. Yet, no critic has interpreted it as the philosophy of *Hamlet*. Perhaps the reason for this neglect is that it is already obvious to us when Hamlet makes his claim for subjectivity that he, more than anyone else in the play, disbelieves and rebels against such a doctrine. The trap laid here in Hamlet's affirmation of moral subjectivism, into which no one has yet fallen, should serve as a warning against similar traps into which critics have fallen when they have pulled certain philosophical remarks out of their dramatic contexts.

Two more examples of dialog that suggest philosophical generalization are:

HAMLET: . . . What a piece of work is a man, how noble in reason, how infinite in faculties, in form and moving, how express and admirable in action, how like an angel in apprehension, how like a god: the beauty of the world; the paragon of animals; and yet to me, what is this quintessence of dust?

(II, 2, 307-312)

ROSENCRANTZ: The cess of majesty
Dies not alone; but like a gulf doth draw
What's near it with it. O, 'tis a massy wheel
Fixed on the summit of the highest mount,
To whose huge spokes ten thousand lesser things
Are mortised and adjoined, which when it falls,
Each small annexment, petty consequence,
Attends the boist'rous ruin. Never alone
Did the king sigh, but with a general groan.

(III, 3, 15-23)

Both Hamlet's speech on man and Rosencrantz' statement on kingship express doctrines that are integral to the general philosophical view of reality as a Chain of

Being. For many critics, Theodore Spencer among them, these two passages culminate in a philosophy of optimism that was articulated by the Elizabethan version of the universe as a Chain of Being. *Hamlet* as a whole is interpreted as the dramatization of the conflict between Elizabethan optimism and pessimism, although the conflict is no longer in the background of the action but is instead inside the hero's consciousness.

Two further related examples of philosophy in the dialog are:

HAMLET: . . . We defy augury. There is special providence in the fall of a sparrow. If it be now, 'tis not to come—if it be not to come, it will be now—if it be not now, yet it will come—the readiness is all. . . .

(V, 2, 217-220)

HAMLET: Let us know
Our indiscretion sometime serves us well,
When our deep plots do pall, and that should learn us
There's a divinity that shapes our ends,
Rough-hew them how we will—

(V, 2, 7-11)

Both these bits of dialog addressed to Horatio beg for religious interpretation, and there have been many critics who have gleaned philosophical readings of the whole of *Hamlet* from these and other passages about the providential nature of the *Hamlet* universe.

Two final examples of dialog that invite philosophical generalization are:

PLAYER KING: What to ourselves in passion we propose,
The passion ending, doth the purpose lose.
The violence of either grief or joy
Their own enactures with themselves destroy,
Where joy most revels, grief doth most lament,
Grief joys, joy grieves, on slender accident.

(III, 2, 193-198)

HAMLET: And blest are those
Whose blood and judgement are so well co-medled,

That they are not a pipe for Fortune's finger
To sound what stop she please: give me that man
That is not passion's slave, and I will wear him
In my heart's core, ay in my heart of heart,
As I do thee.

(III, 2, 66-72)

The interpretation given these last two philosophical passages is the interpretation I first wish to consider. In Lily Campbell's book *Shakespeare's Tragic Heroes: Slaves of Passion,* the drama *Hamlet,* like the other major Shakespearean tragedies, is considered fundamentally a study in passion. Indeed, Miss Campbell claims in each of the tragedies the hero is dominated by one passion, which Shakespeare analyzed in accordance with the medical and moral doctrines of his day. The passions are love and hatred, desire and aversion, pleasure and grief, hope and despair, courage and fear, and anger. They are located in the appetitive part of the human soul where they relate intimately to the four humors: blood, choler, phlegm, and melancholy, because the passions influence and are influenced by the humors.

For example, each of the three sons in *Hamlet* is called upon to mourn his father and to avenge a wrong suffered by his father. Each son's response to grief is determined by his individual temperament: Fortinbras, a northerner, is phlegmatic or sanguine; Laertes, a southerner in his love of France, is choleric and hot-complexioned; and Hamlet, also a northerner, is sanguine or phlegmatic, at least before the play opens. Hamlet's development from the sanguine to the sanguine adust or, as it was called, the "melancholy adust," is brought about by excessive grief. It is this tendency toward excess that creates the constant conflict between the passions and the rational part of the soul; it is this conflict that gives rise to the moral problem of how men are to control their passion by reason.

The whole of Elizabethan tragedy is an attempt to present and explain this moral problem by showing a just and computative God who punishes those whose sin and folly are self-induced through the exercise of passion. Dramatic tragedy, because it is imitation that pleases as it teaches, serves as an effective exemplar of "how to avoid ruin and misery by avoiding the loose and ungoverned passions that lead thereto." [3] Consequently, *Hamlet*, because it is a study in the passion of grief, is an example of moral philosophy that delightfully and spiritedly teaches us how to avoid sin and ruin. Indeed, the play is ". . . constructed to show the profound truth of its dominant idea": [4]

> What to ourselves in passion we propose,
> The passion ending, doth the purpose lose,
> The violence of either grief or joy
> Their own enactures with themselves destroy,
> Where joy most revels, grief doth most lament;
> Grief joys, joy grieves, on slender accident.
> (III, 2, 193-198)

These words of the Player King Miss Campbell glosses as the central idea of a play about a man ". . . impelled by passion to revenge and yet through excess of passion having the cause of his passion blurred in his memory." [5]

But grief is more than diversified in *Hamlet;* it is also tied to the moral philosophy of the age. The main problem is consolation in grief: how men accept sorrow when it comes to them. In *Hamlet* Shakespeare contrasts a grief that seeks consolation with a grief that remains inconsolable and results either in dullness and loss of memory, the sin of sloth, or in hasty anger and rashness, the sin of ire. Fortinbras exemplifies grief consoled by reason; Laertes demonstrates inconsolable grief that results in anger, the sin of ire; and Hamlet embraces an inconsolable grief that culminates in his dullness, the sin of sloth. Hamlet's grief results in a melancholy adust and, in effect, provides a case study of a man who will not yield to the consolation of reason, as urged by Claudius and Gertrude, in the moderation of his passion of grief. For this he is justly punished. Ophelia reflects another facet of this problem, for grief in her is exemplified in its most intemperate form, one that leads to madness and destruction. She, Hamlet, and Laertes represent venial sin, that is, passion undirected by reason; for this they are destroyed but not damned. Claudius and Gertrude, on the other hand, represent mortal sin, that is, passion in control of and perverting reason; they are destroyed and damned. Fortinbras and Horatio exemplify reason victorious over passion. Hamlet himself sums up Horatio as one in whom "blood and judgement are so well commingled" that he is no slave of passion, no pipe of fortune to play upon. "And this is but to say," Miss Campbell concludes, "that those who balance passion by reason are not Fortune's puppets. And such is the lesson of tragedy." [6]

Miss Campbell's critical method and interpretation are a paradigm of philosophical intrusion in *Hamlet*. She picks out one passage, her nugget of "profound truth," abstracts it from its dramatic context, paraphrases it by reducing its meaning to the one idea that passion in excess gives rise to sin, and then reduces the whole play to a series of variations on this idea. The rest of the dialog, the entirety of the action, and the philosophical significance of the play must revolve around this one general idea of the need to balance passion with reason. Indeed, *Hamlet* for her is a case study in philosophy, teaching us how to caution ourselves against divine punishment.

Reduction generally leads to distortion, and Miss

Campbell's attempt is no exception. Her reading necessitates a basic perversion of *Hamlet* and Hamlet's grief which is the *donnée* she starts with.

Miss Campbell associates Hamlet with Fortinbras and Laertes—all grief-stricken over a father lost and wronged. But surely Hamlet is grieving for more than this. Remember his first soliloquy:

> O most wicked speed . . . to post
> With such dexterity to incestuous sheets!
> It is not, nor it cannot come to good,
> But break my heart, for I must hold my tongue.
>
> (I, 2, 156-159)

These lines certainly express a grief that goes beyond a father's death and includes a mother's incest; hence, Hamlet's grief calls for more than consolation for a father lost and wronged. So we must ask Miss Campbell, once we comprehend the true nature of Hamlet's grief, if the moral philosophers of the Elizabethan age, or of any age for that matter, have a clear case of the sin of sloth in Hamlet's inconsolable grief over a father murdered and a mother whored? Miss Campbell's method of abstraction forecloses on the full and horrible nature of Hamlet's sorrow as he reveals it to us. Given that sorrow, for which Hamlet is not responsible, the play cannot be reduced to an exemplary study in the avoidance of divine retribution, without making a moral mockery of man's deepest filial feelings.

Similar to Miss Campbell's reduction of the play to one or more selections of dialog or soliloquy is the equally dangerous attempt to ascribe to another aspect of the language the philosophy of the play. Caroline Spurgeon, in her epoch-making book *Shakespeare's Imagery and What It Tells Us*, argues that the center of every Shakespearean drama is its dominant imagery. It is this poetic imagery that ". . . gives quality, creates atmosphere and conveys emotion in a way no precise description, however clear and accurate, can possibly do." [7] For example, in *Hamlet* the pervasive atmosphere is created by ". . . the number of images of sickness, disease or blemish of the body, in the play." [8] The dominant imagery is that of an ulcer or tumor that expresses the sickness of Denmark itself. She enumerates these images: "blister," "sick soul," "thought-sick," "mildew'd ear," "mote," "vicious mole," "galled chilblain," "probed wound," and "purgation." Rottenness, physical, mental, and political, is the striking quality of these images. Thus, she says:

> To Shakespeare's pictorial imagination, therefore, the problem in *Hamlet* is not predominantly that of will and reason, of a mind too philosophic or a nature temperamentally unfitted to act quickly; he sees it pictorially *not as the problem of an individual at all*, but as something greater and even more mysterious, as a *condition* for which the individual himself is apparently not responsible, any more than the sick man is to blame for the infection which strikes and devours him, but which, nevertheless, in its course and development, impartially and relentlessly, annihilates him and others, innocent and guilty alike. That is the tragedy of *Hamlet*, as it is perhaps the chief tragic mystery of life.[9]

For Miss Spurgeon, then, the philosophy of *Hamlet* is its imagistic affirmation of the destructive natural condition of man, the tragic fact of life. As profound as this claim is, or as accurate as her classification of the imagery of *Hamlet* may be, the reduction of the philosophy of *Hamlet* to the imagery that expresses a fundamental truth about life does not do justice to the whole play, especially to the quality of moral responsibility shared by the major characters.

Nor does her concentration on the imagery do justice

to the role of the imagery itself. For as Clemen in *The Development of Shakespeare's Imagery* shows, *Hamlet* cannot be interpreted in terms of its imagery alone, but the imagery must be related to the whole play: the plot, characters, and theme. Miss Spurgeon's statistical method of collecting and classifying images and her consequent isolation of them from their exact dramatic contexts violate the organic role imagery plays in the drama. The imagery discloses no ultimate pattern beneath the characters and plot, rather imagery is but one contributing element among many others. The plot, not the tragic fact of life, Clemen points out, dictates the imagery: the murder of King Hamlet and the incest of Gertrude give rise to the imagery of disease, infection, and corruption. However, as the drama unfolds, ". . . imagery and action continually play into each other's hands and we see how the term 'dramatic imagery' gains a new significance." [10] Hamlet's images, Clemen says, are the most striking in the play. They are not so much similes or metaphors as they are imaginative translations of real things and persons. They are keen, penetrating observations of reality, referring as they do to its most ordinary aspects—trades, callings, objects, games. Indeed, Hamlet is unique in the play for his spontaneous and unpremeditated images, which reveal him to be no mere abstract thinker or dreamer.

Clemen examines the much-discussed image:

> HAMLET: And thus the native hue of resolution
> Is sicklied o'er with the pale cast of thought,
> And enterprises of great pitch and moment
> With this regard their currents turn awry,
> And lose the name of action.
>
> (III, 1, 84-88)

and concludes that the traditional interpretation of this passage—that reflection hinders action—is wrong:

For Hamlet does not say "reflection hinders action," he simply utters this image. The fact that he does not utter that general maxim, but this image, makes all the difference. For this image is the unique and specific form of expression of the thought underlying it, it cannot be separated from it. If we say "reflection hinders action," we make a false generalization; we replace a specific formulation by an apothegm. And thereby we eradicate in this passage that quality which is peculiarly Shakespeare's or, what is more, peculiarly Hamlet's. Here the image does not serve the purpose of merely casting a decorative cloak about the thought; it is much rather an intrinsic part of the thought.[11]

The adage "reflection hinders action" implies that action and reflection are two opposing moral principles. But in Hamlet's image, ". . . 'native hue of resolution' suggests that Shakespeare viewed resolution as an innate human quality, not as a moral virtue to be consciously striven after." [12] Thought and action are related in Shakespeare ". . . not as an opposition between two abstract principles between which a free choice is possible, but as an unavoidable condition of human nature." [13]

Although it has been established that the philosophy of *Hamlet* is not contained in the imagery alone, nor can it be isolated in the dialog or soliloquies, some critics still contend that it can be secured in the plot. For example, Francis Fergusson's fundamental thesis about *Hamlet* is that the main action—"the basic situation"—of the play is the attempt to find and destroy the "hidden imposthume" of Denmark. Hence, it is the welfare of Denmark, not the hero's plight, that is central. The whole action is based on the time's being out of joint. Everything reflects this uneasiness; consequently, *Hamlet* must be seen as a series of shifting perspectives on this analog. Moreover, since everyone in the play has a share in the main action—the welfare of Denmark—there is nothing irrelevant in it.

Fergusson, thus, divides the action of the play into a prolog (Act I, scenes 1, 2, 3) in which the malady of Denmark is brought out, the agons or conflicts and contrasts (Act I, scenes 4, 5; Act II; Act III, scene 1) in which an attempt is made to identify and destroy the malady, the climax, peripety, and recognition (Act III, scenes 2, 3, 4) in which the hidden imposthume is opened, the pathos or sparagmos (Act IV) in which all the suffering is culminated, and the epiphany or collective revelation (Act V) in which the illness of Denmark is perceived by all.

Hamlet, furthermore, as a multiple-plot structure, parallels *The Odyssey* rather than Greek or French classical tragedy, for *The Odyssey* is also a series of analogs on one major theme—the attempt to return home. Like Homer, Shakespeare composes by analogy, not by emotional or conceptual progression. The anagoge or ultimate meaning, which is Denmark as it mirrors the world, is present in all the analogical relations within the play: the ironic parallels formed by tragic and comic motifs, the father-son relationships, and the male-female relationships.

But to grasp the total meaning of *Hamlet* we must also see the main action as a manifestation of the ancient myth and ritual pattern of human experience. *Hamlet* is a celebration of the mystery of human life, and it is this celebration rather than form that ties the play inextricably to Greek tragedy and the ancient ritual. There are profound parallels in *Hamlet* and *Oedipus Rex*. In fact, for Fergusson, the main difference between the two plays is that one comes at the beginning and the other at the end of the tradition of theater as ritual. In both plays, the royal personage is associated with pollution; there is invocation for well-being; and there is the interweaving of the individual and society. In *Hamlet*, the rituals show forth the main action; they are ". . . lamps lighting the rottenness of Denmark." [14] From the beginning when the guards change to the end when Hamlet is borne like a soldier by four captains, there are rituals that function to focus attention on the body politic and ceremoniously invoke well-being. Indeed, the play scene is the center of the drama. "It has a ritual aspect, it is Hamlet's most ambitious improvisation, and it is the climax and peripety of the whole complex plot-scheme." [15] "It reveals the malady of the regime in all its ambiguity, mystery, and spreading ramifications. . . . It catches more than the conscience of the King." [16] It represents the hidden crime, the incestuous theft, the usurpation. Altogether this scene functions as an anagoge of human weakness.

As the traditional scapegoat-hero, Hamlet is the appointed victim to cleanse the scourge of a sick society:

> Hamlet is apparently thought of as undergoing a similar [to Oedipus] transformation, from hero to scapegoat, from "the expectancy and rose of the fair state" to the distracted, suffering witness and victim of Act V.[17]

The other characters also are placed in the ritualistic scheme Fergusson finds in the play. His most important observation is on Fortinbras, who is referred to early in the play as a threat to a (corrupt) regime, is seen briefly in Act IV, scene 4, and is recognized at the very end of the play as the future legitimate monarch. ". . . In the scheme of the whole the role of Fortinbras, though it is very economically developed, is of major importance." [18] He is a symbol of spiritual rebirth after the cleansing of the scourge; consequently, he, too, functions as part of the ancient myth and ritual pattern of drama, the celebration of the mystery of human life.

So much by way of an all-too-brief account of Fergusson's reading of *Hamlet*. For him the philosophy of *Hamlet*, as it is embodied and re-enacted in the plot of the play, is the religious affirmation of the cycle of human life, from birth, struggle, and death to renewal: from Claudius, through Hamlet, to Fortinbras.

It seems to me that there is much to be said for Fergusson's interpretation of *Hamlet*. His emphases on the unity of the action, the multiple-plot, the search for the hidden imposthume, the symbolic value of Fortinbras, and even the purgatorial role of Hamlet are convincing. But that the whole play adds up to a Renaissance version of the ancient myth and ritual pattern in which the mystery cycle of life, death, and renewal is celebrated, or that Hamlet is a mere scapegoat-hero, ". . . a witness and a sufferer for the hidden truth of the human condition," [19] is not satisfying, primarily because such a reading does not do justice to the important secular and skeptical strands of the play and its hero. Fergusson's interpretation, like other univocal readings, forecloses on the undeniable complexities within the drama that make it much more than a transformation of *Oedipus Rex*. Even if Fergusson be correct on the nature of the plot, the attempt to reduce the philosophy and the meaning of the whole play to his analysis of the plot leaves much unaccounted for.

The failures of Miss Campbell, Miss Spurgeon, and Mr. Fergusson to pluck out the heart of the philosophy of *Hamlet* from its dialog, imagery, and plot suggest that perhaps *Hamlet* has no underlying philosophy. E. E. Stoll says as much. And whatever we may think of his reading of the play, we must allow that it has the decided merit of bodily rejecting philosophy, before the intruder crosses the threshold of *Hamlet*. Stoll has written much on *Hamlet*, but his thesis has never changed. The play is a revenge tragedy or heroic romance, pure and simple, which makes no philosophical or psychological claims about the world. It is in the great tradition derived from Seneca and sponsored in the Renaissance especially by Thomas Kyd. It is drama of intrigue, blood, and fate in which the hero remains free from defect or tragic flaw throughout the play and attains his appointed revenge. Stoll supports this thesis by an appeal to both external and internal evidence. His external evidence is that the play was regarded as a typical revenge tragedy from its first appearance to the late eighteenth century. Readers and spectators during this early period complained of the defects of the play, but no one complained of psychological deficiencies in the hero.

The internal evidence is the dramatic. Every relevant datum of the text, Stoll claims, supports his contention that *Hamlet* is a revenge tragedy, not a psychological study. First is the delay. Stoll does not deny that Hamlet delays but he does deny that the delay has psychological significance. The delay functions, as it had from the Greeks on, in the epical tradition, not to accentuate the defects of the hero, but to make the deed momentous when it comes. Because tradition and the old *Hamlet* story required the delay, Shakespeare simply relied on established devices. Though woefully misconstrued by later critics, the hero's self-reproaches and exhortations function not as character traits, but as dramatic reminders to the audience that Hamlet's main business, though retarded, is not lost to view. Indeed, the self-reproaches, although they contain execrations, interrogations, even lacerations, serve as exhortations and, finally, as exculpation. Even the Ghost's reminder to Hamlet,

Do not forget! this visitation
Is but to whet thy almost blunted purpose—
                    (III, 4, 110-111)

is exhortation, not judgment on Hamlet's character. The highly emotional scenes—the cellarage, the nunnery, the play, the graveyard—are not pathological either, for they are natural enough in the dramatic circumstances. These scenes serve to enhance the emotional pitch and form part of the action; they are art as artifice, not as psychology. Finally, that Hamlet is a heroic figure can be inferred from the fact that no character, except himself and the Ghost, reproaches him and, more importantly, because the end of the play, which is "one of your surest indexes of your dramatist's thought," [20] contains nothing but praise for Hamlet and not even a hint of dereliction from Horatio, who should know.

Stoll's interpretation and his wholesale dismissal of both philosophy and psychology in the play rest, of course, on the plausibility of his treatment of the delay. And if this is not convincing, perhaps we can turn to the character of Hamlet for the philosophy of the play. It is Dover Wilson who best counters Stoll's assertion that Hamlet's self-reproaches are exculpation.

. . . That [Stoll's] thesis is moonshine any unprejudiced reader of the soliloquy in 4.4. may see for himself. Not that the evidence of the soliloquies by any means stands alone. Hamlet's sense of frustration, of infirmity of purpose, of character inhibited from meeting the demands of destiny, of the futility of life in general and action in particular, finds utterance in nearly every word he says. His melancholy and his procrastination are all of a piece, and cannot be disentangled. Moreover, his feelings are shared and expressed by other characters also. The note of 'heart-sickness' is struck by the sentry Francisco nine lines from the beginning of the play . . . In short that "the native hue of resolution/Is sicklied o'er with the pale cast of thought," is not merely the constant burden of Hamlet's meditation but the key-note of the whole dramatic symphony.[21]

Much of the tradition, at least from Coleridge to Bradley, has thought that the philosophy of *Hamlet* is in the character of the hero.

Hamlet was the play, or rather Hamlet himself was the character, in the intuition and exposition of which I first made my turn for philosophical criticism. . . .[22]

So wrote Coleridge in 1819, some twenty years after his famous "turn" in criticism. Since this pronouncement, the view that Coleridge is concerned only with character portrayal in *Hamlet* and the whole of Shakespeare's dramas has prevailed. Nothing could be further from the truth. Coleridge's critical interests in Shakespearean drama range from characterization to metaphysical insight, thereby covering the topics of language, unity of feeling, thematic development, and plot. Indeed, his penetrating remark that "Shakespeare shewed great judgement in his first scenes; they contained the germ of the ruling passion which was to be developed hereafter" [23] corroborates the diversity of his interests. Even in his critical remarks on *Hamlet*, fragmentary as they are, Coleridge perceives more in the play than most critics perceive: his observations on the language of the opening scene, Hamlet's wit, the contrast between the playlet and the rest of the play, the judicious introductions of Hamlet and Laertes in the second scene, the sure handling of the Ghost, and the way in which Hamlet's mind operates are cases in point. Where else in Shakespearean criticism is there anything that can match the aesthetic power, for example, of Coleridge's reading of the opening scene?

The language is familiar: no poetic description of night, no elaborate information conveyed by one speaker to another. . . . It is the language of *sensation* among men who feared no charge of effeminacy for feeling what they felt no want of resolution to bear. Yet the armour, the dead silence, the watchfulness that first interrupts it, the welcome relief of guard, the cold, the broken expressions as of a man's compelled attention to bodily feelings allowed no man—all excellently accord with and prepare for the after gradual rise into tragedy. . . .

The preparation *informative* of the audience is just as much as was precisely necessary: how gradual first, and with the uncertainty appertaining to a question— What, has *this thing* appeared *again* to-night. Even the word "again" has its credibilizing effect.[24]

No, Hamlet is primary in *Hamlet,* not because Coleridge reduces the drama to characterization, but because, for him, Hamlet *is* primary in *Hamlet.* Shakespeare, Coleridge says, never wrote anything without design. In the character of Hamlet, "he intended to portray a person in whose view the external world, and all its incidents and objects, were comparatively dim and of no interest in themselves, and which began to interest only when they were reflected in the mirror of his mind." [25]

Hamlet is called upon to act, to avenge his murdered father; he does not act. Instead he reasons and broods, rationalizes and reproaches himself, "while the whole energy of his resolution evaporates in these reproaches." Yet Hamlet refrains from action not because of cowardice, "but merely from that aversion to action which prevails among such as have a world in themselves." [26] Hence, from a philosophical point of view, Hamlet exemplifies ". . . the moral necessity of a due balance between our attention to outward objects and our meditation on inward thoughts—a due balance between the real and the imaginary world. In Hamlet this balance does not exist. . . ." [27] From Hamlet's opening line, "A little more than kin, and less than kind," in which Coleridge says Hamlet expresses his contempt for Claudius as well as his ". . . superfluous activity of mind, a sort of playing with a thread or watch chain or snuff box," [28] through the soliloquies, indeed, up until the very end, Hamlet remains in words all resolution but in action all words.

Coleridge sums up the philosophy of the play as it is embodied in the character of Hamlet:

> Shakespeare wished to impress upon us the truth, that action is the chief end of existence—that no faculties of intellect, however brilliant, can be considered valuable, or indeed otherwise than as misfortunes, if they withdraw us from, or render us repugnant to action, and lead us to think and think of doing, until the time has elapsed when we can do anything effectually." [29]

For Coleridge, then, Hamlet is central in the play; his inaction, pervasive in him, is caused by his excessive reflectiveness; and this undue imbalance between action and thought dramatizes the moral philosophy of the play that too much philosophy, that is, philosophy without action, is immoral.

Now, Coleridge's reading of *Hamlet*, probably the most influential in the entire history of criticism, has itself been challenged on all major points by many later critics, not least of all by A. C. Bradley who, although he agrees with Coleridge that Hamlet is central in the play, that Hamlet's delay—but not total inaction—pervades him, and that the philosophy of the play is to be found in the hero, disagrees with Coleridge on the cause of the delay and especially on the philosophical significance of Hamlet himself. Hamlet delays, but, Bradley argues, not because he is thought-sick, which he is not, but rather because he is in a profound state of melancholy, a state which has been induced both by his predisposition toward brooding and obsession with the mood of the moment and the shock of his mother's hasty, indecent remarriage. In his classic, *Shakespearean Tragedy*, Bradley spells out his theory in magnificent detail. Of course, his own hypothesis about Hamlet's delay has been challenged on textual as well as on purely logical grounds, reduced almost necessarily to the Freudian hypothesis of Ernest Jones, for whom the vacillation is due to a rather stiff double dose of the Oedipal complex, and dismissed entirely, along with all other univocal explanations of Hamlet's behavior, by Dover Wilson, who insists that Hamlet was intended by Shakespeare to remain a mystery:

> In fine, we were never intended to reach the heart of the mystery. That it has a heart is an illusion; the mystery itself is an illusion; Hamlet is an illusion. The secret that lies behind it all is not Hamlet's, but Shakespeare's: the technical devices he employed to create this supreme illusion of a great and mysterious character, who is at once mad and the sanest of geniuses, at once a procrastinator and a vigorous man of action, at once a miserable failure and the most adorable of heroes. The character of Hamlet, like the appearance of his successive impersonators on the stage, is a matter of "make-up." [30]

Bradley, however, admits that the philosophy of *Hamlet* is not in Hamlet the philosopher, Hamlet the procrastinator, or Hamlet the melancholic. It is in Hamlet the tragic hero.

Hamlet alone is tragic in *Hamlet*, not because he dies for a valiant cause, or because he is a slave of passion, or because he is a relatively good man who ruins himself through his tragic flaw, but because in his struggle with the forces of evil his spiritual greatness is destroyed irretrievably. For Bradley, the tragic fact in the world is this ultimate, unexplainable, non-justifiable self-waste of spiritual goodness in its struggle against evil:

We remain confronted with the inexplicable fact, or the no less inexplicable appearance, of a world travailing for perfection, but bringing to birth, together with glorious good, an evil which it is able to overcome only by self-torture and self-waste. And this fact or appearance is tragedy.[31]

However, only Hamlet exemplifies this mystery of good's expelling evil and being destroyed in the very process. Coleridge, therefore, according to Bradley, is wrong in reducing the philosophy of *Hamlet* to a moral maxim about thought and action. For Bradley the philosophy of *Hamlet* is the dramatization of a perennial truth about man: that man lives in a world where good can vanquish evil and yet be wasted. There is no acceptable explanation of this fact. It remains a mystery.

Many critics agree with Bradley that the philosophy of *Hamlet* is in the tragedy of the hero but they reject Bradley's definition of the tragic as the self-waste of spiritual good. This disagreement turns on the supposed essence of the tragic, which each of these disputing critics claims to state truly. But this issue, it seems to me, cannot be settled in any true or false manner, because there is no such thing as the essence of the tragic. If the philosophy of *Hamlet* be identified with the tragic in Hamlet and the tragic in Hamlet be defined in terms of the essence of tragedy, an essence that is non-existent, then the philosophy of *Hamlet* cannot be determined at all. But I believe it can be determined by turning from dialog, soliloquy, imagery, character, and tragedy to that which served so well in the discussions of *Candide* and *Anna Karenina*, namely, the tone of the play. Our best critical guide here is E. M. W. Tillyard. His essay on "Hamlet" in *Shakespeare's Problem Plays* is one of the few enlightening pieces of criticism of the play since Bradley.

For Tillyard, the tragic is not primary in *Hamlet*. He

distinguishes between three kinds of tragedy: suffering, sacrificial purgation, and regeneration. The third, he says, is the "centrally tragic." Both *King Lear* and *Othello* are tragic in this fundamental sense; *Hamlet* is not since Hamlet never regenerates himself. *Hamlet* is tragic only in the first two senses, but even in these the tragic is ". . . not the principal quality." [32] Rather, for Tillyard it is the tone that is central in *Hamlet:*

> . . . the sheer wealth and vigour and brilliance of all the things that happen . . . Simply as a play of things happening, of one event being bred out of another, and of each event being described with appropriate and unwearied brilliance, *Hamlet* is supreme . . . One is tempted to call *Hamlet* the greatest display of sheer imaginative vitality in literary form that a man has so far achieved.[33]

If, Tillyard continues, we distinguish between content and form, or recognize what for Aristotle was the difference between imitation and harmony, in the sense in which, say, *Othello* emphasizes the form or ordering of experience rather than the content of it, *Hamlet* ". . . is best understood as a play less of ordering than of sheer explication or presentation, as a play presenting the utmost variety of human experience in the largest possible cosmic setting." Hamlet himself serves in the play to render evident ". . . the wonder and variety of all human experience." [34] Thus, *Hamlet* ceases to be a tragedy and becomes instead a "problem play," for:

> When sheer explication, or abundance of things presented, takes first place, then we leave the realm of tragedy for that of the problem play. Here it is the problems themselves, their richness, their interest, and their diversity, and not their solution or significant arrangement that come first.[35]

Now, much of Tillyard's analysis is open to debate; for example, that the regenerative is the centrally tragic, that *Hamlet* is a tragedy of suffering and sacrificial purgation, that the tragic in *Hamlet* is not primary, that *Hamlet* is essentially a problem play, and that the tone is primary in *Hamlet*. But what is not challengeable, indeed, what is quite indubitable, is his presentation of the tone of the play. Tillyard's description is a necessary reminder of what most critics have utterly forgotten since Dr. Johnson's remark that variety is the distinguishing excellence of *Hamlet*. The tone establishes the beginning as well as the end of any attempt to provide a reading of the philosophy in *Hamlet*. I do not wish to say that the tone is primary in *Hamlet*, but only that it is there, a pervasive quality or *donnée* as obviously and undeniably present as the imagery of rottenness or the blood and guts of melodrama.

There is, however, more to be said about the tone of *Hamlet* than that its range of presented or represented experiences is great, vigorous, brilliant, and vital. As these qualities establish, the tone is also life-enhancing, if I may borrow a term from Berenson. That is, the quality of the sheer love of life, of being alive, is shared by all, including the melancholic Hamlet. Hamlet can gossip with the players, remind them of the rudiments of their craft, partake of the artist's ecstasy over a good play well done; and he can jest with Polonius, the King, and the gravediggers. Of course it is true that he complains to Rosencrantz and Guildenstern that he has of late, he knows not why, lost his mirth; yet minutes before he has pulled off one of his delightful bits of bawdiness in his burlesque of Fortune as a strumpet in whose privates Rosencrantz and Guildenstern enjoy her favors. Hamlet has lost his mirth, but clearly not quite all of it. He can still joke obscenely, yet harmlessly, with Ophelia later in the play. His wit, often expressed for the sheer love of it, is present throughout. Certainly he is bitter and depressed, but the natural delight in wit and humor shines through the darkness.

Mystery, too, pervades much of the play. Many have commented on the predominantly interrogative mood of the drama—all its questioning, doubt, and uncertainty. Harry Levin even reads "question" as the key word of the play. To be or not to be? Is the Ghost an honest one? Is Ophelia honest? Is Gertrude bestial? What is the true nature of man? Why do I delay? These are among the questions of the play.

The variety and the wonder, along with the woe, imply a kind of irreducible complexity of human experience, the idea that man lives in a universe which is inexhaustively vast—from the "majestical roof fretted with golden fire" to the "quintessence of dust." And it is a universe whose vastness reflects itself only in man's infinitesimal comprehension of it. We live in a world in which we can formulate the questions, but we can hardly answer them. Hamlet cannot even answer why he delays. He knows not "seems," he says, but neither does he know what is. It is in this aspect of the tone—the irreducible complexity of human experience as it mirrors man's condition—that I find the philosophy of *Hamlet*. Paradoxically, it is philosophy that rejects the very possibility of a philosophy of man and the universe. In the traditional sense in which philosophy is the attempt to reduce the complexity of experience and the world to a formula, to provide answers to the great questions about the meaning of life, to pluck out the heart of the mystery of the universe, *Hamlet* shows, through its over-all quality of irreducible complexity, that the formula cannot be secured; consequently, philosophy itself functions as an intruder on the human situation. *Hamlet*, then, *is* a celebration of the mystery of human life, not in the myth and ritual pattern, but in the more basic secular pattern of life as a series of questions to which there are no certain answers. Life is and remains a mystery. Hamlet's delay and his tragedy instance that mystery. As artist, Shakespeare dramatizes the mystery; as philosophical artist, he also dramatizes the denial of any convincing solution to the mystery. In effect, in *Hamlet*, Shakespeare shows us that man lives, questions, affirms, doubts, and dies. The rest is silence.

IV. *A la Recherche du Temps Perdu:*

PHILOSOPHY AS ARTISTIC VISION

At the end of Proust's novel, the title of which is inadequately translated as *Remembrance of Things Past*, the narrator, who is Marcel himself, has just left a sanatorium, uncured of his illness. His doubts about his literary talents and the value of literature are stronger than ever. During the railway journey back to Paris, he tries to reawaken his feelings for nature, only to be overcome by a boredom that reinforces his doubts: nature and human beings can no longer inspire him.

Upon his arrival in Paris he finds awaiting him an invitation to an afternoon reception at the Prince de Guermantes'. For various reasons, but especially because he hopes his presence there will bring back his childhood from the depths of his memory, he accepts the invitation. On the day of the reception Marcel orders a carriage and rides over some badly paved streets that lead through the Champs Élysées to the Avenue du Bois, where the Prince has built his new mansion. The streets are those Marcel had taken with Françoise many years ago as they walked to the Champs Élysées where Marcel met and fell in love with Gilberte. During the ride Marcel feels himself "being slowly lifted towards the silent peaks of memory." [1] He leaves his carriage, walks, and meets the Baron de Charlus, who is partially recovered from a recent stroke. The Baron has aged considerably; his silver hair and beard give him the majesty of a Lear. They talk; the Baron triumphantly announces the deaths of many relatives and friends whom he has outlived. Marcel leaves the Baron, returns to his carriage, and descends again a little before his destination. His lassitude is all-pervasive; the reception now strikes him as pure frivolity and acceptable only because there is nothing else to occupy him. He enters the courtyard of the Guermantes home. Distracted, he does not notice an approaching carriage. A servant calls out; Marcel steps back, stumbling against some uneven paving stones. He recovers his balance. With one foot on a stone lower than the next, the moment of illumination—the Proustian epiphany—begins:

> . . . Sometimes illumination comes to our rescue at the very moment when all seems lost; we have knocked at every door and they open on nothing until, at last, we stumble unconsciously against the only one through which we can enter the kingdom we have sought in vain a hundred years—and it opens.
> [For in the very instant of the stepping on the stones] . . . my discouragement disappeared and I was possessed by the same felicity which at different moments of my life had given me the view of trees which seemed familiar to me during the drive round Balbec, the view of the belfries of Martinville, the savour of the madeleine dipped in my tea and so many other sensations of which I have spoken and which Vinteuil's last works had seemed to synthesise.[2]

Marcel's doubts about literature and his literary talents vanish. This time he must find the cause of his felicity, a task he had always postponed before. Then, once more, without any conscious effort, Marcel recalls a similar sensation of uneven stones experienced in the Baptistry of St. Mark in Venice. His immediate sensation, literally stumbled upon, has involuntarily called up a similar one which links the present with still other sensations associated with Venice. Marcel is overcome. Nevertheless, he pays his visit, entering the house while one of the concert pieces is being performed. He is ushered into the little library to await the conclusion of the entertainment. Two additional illuminations occur: one touched off by a servant's spoon knocking on a plate, the other, by a starched napkin. All three sensations and their effects produce the same felicity. For the first time in his life Marcel forces himself to determine the cause of this sudden joy:

> And I began to discover the cause by comparing those varying happy impressions which had the common quality of being felt simultaneously at the actual moment and at a distance in time, because of which common quality the noise of the spoon upon the plate, the unevenness of the paving-stones, the taste of the madeleine, imposed the past upon the present and made me hesitate as to which time I was existing in. Of a truth, the being within me which sensed this impression, sensed what it had in common in former days and now, sensed its extra-temporal character, a being which only appeared when through the medium of the identity of present and past, it found itself in the only setting in which it could exist and enjoy the essence of things, that is, outside Time.[3]

The depths are penetrated; Marcel has gone beyond appearances to their ultimate reality—from mere sensations which occur in time to their essences which exist out of time. Reality, he now sees, consists in these essences and can be discovered by the writer only when he:

> . . . takes two different objects, posits their relationship, the analogue in the world of art to the only relationship of causal law in the world of science, and encloses it within the circle of fine style . . . [when]

> . . . he fuses a quality common to two sensations,
> extracts their essence and in order to withdraw them
> from the contingencies of time, unites them in a
> metaphor, thus chaining them together with the in-
> definable bond of a verbal alliance.[4]

Art, Marcel realizes, is the only means of regaining lost
time as well as transcending time altogether. This unifica-
tion of the past and the present by means of a language
that is out of time is a matter of artistic vision, rendered
possible only by intuition. And intuition is made possible
only by much suffering.

> For . . . it is only while we are suffering that our
> thoughts, in a constant state of agitation and change,
> cause the depths within us to surge as in a tempest
> to a height where we see that they are subject to laws
> which, until then, we could not observe, because the
> calm of happiness left those depths undisturbed. . . .
> One might almost say that works of literature are like
> artesian wells, the deeper the suffering, the higher they
> rise.[5]

But he also realizes that intuition is not enough; the artist
needs the aid of the intellect as well. Our experiences are:

> . . . like certain negatives which show black until they
> are placed under a lamp and they too must be looked
> at from the back: we do not know what a thing is until
> we have approached it with our intelligence.[6]

The butler arrives to inform Marcel that he can now
enter the drawing room. Marcel does so, seeing before
him many of his old acquaintances: the Prince de Guermantes; the Princesse, his wife, who was the former
vehemently anti-aristocratic Mme Verdurin; Bloch, who
has also changed his name, but not through marriage;
Rachel, who is now at the height of her theatrical career
and whom Marcel had known first as a prostitute and

then as the mistress of his dear friend, Robert de Saint-Loup; Odette; her daughter, Gilberte; and Gilberte's daughter. The years have left their mark on these people, but Marcel does not realize this until someone laughs at his remark about his being a young man. The sudden recognition that he, too, is old forces him to accept another dimension of time:

> The cruel discovery I had now made regarding the lapse of Time could only enrich my ideas and add to the material of my book. Since I had decided that it could not consist only of pure intuitions, namely those beyond Time, amongst the verities with which I intended to frame them, those which are concerned with Time, Time, in which men, societies, and nations bathe and change, would have an important place.[7]

Marcel's final reflection on time is to wish that he have enough time left to live so that he can complete the novel born within him today:

> If at least, time enough were allotted to me to accomplish my work, I would not fail to mark it with the seal of Time, the idea of which imposed itself upon me with so much force to-day, and I would therein describe men, if need be, as monsters occupying a place in Time infinitely more important than the restricted one reserved for them in space, a place, on the contrary, prolonged immeasurably since, simultaneously touching widely separated years and the distant periods they have lived through—between which so many days have ranged themselves—they stand like giants immersed in Time.[8]

So ends Proust's novel. And so, too, does it begin with Marcel's reflections in the opening pages of *Swann's Way* on Combray and his childhood. The whole of the novel is a magnificent threnody on time, life, and love, all seem-

ingly lost and wasted, but whose very themes culminate
in the epithalamium of art and reality in the last volume,
Time Regained. For Proust has not so much created a
world as he has written its obituary, which neither time
nor death can touch because they can never meet it.

The last volume reveals for the first time what it is that
Marcel, as narrator-hero of the novel, is seeking and seeking in vain until the day of his triple illumination. Even
as a child in Combray, Marcel experiences that mixture
of happiness at sudden impressionism and misery at his
impotence in finding "a philosophic theme for some great
literary work." [9] One day he sees the twin steeples of
Martinville, ascertains and notes their shapes, studies their
changes of aspects, and watches the sun play upon their
surfaces. His response to these appearances is joyous, but
he also senses that he has missed something. He frames his
impressions in words. His essay intoxicates him:

> . . . I found such a sense of happiness, felt that it had
> so entirely relieved my mind of the obsession of the
> steeples, and of the mystery which they concealed, that,
> as though I myself were a hen and had just laid an egg,
> I began to sing at the top of my voice.[10]

The Marcel of the novel spends his whole life looking for
a site where he can build a cathedral upon which to secure
his vision of those steeples of Martinville; at long last he
finds the site in the courtyard and the library of the
Prince de Guermantes.

But Marcel does something more: his search for the
metaphors that would bring him the happiness of philosophical truth is rooted in his search for those phrases that
would bring him once again the assuagement of anxiety
which his mother's reading had brought him long ago
on that crucial night when he was deprived of his mother's kiss. Swann has just left; Marcel is hysterical; his
mother comes up the stairs; Marcel throws himself at her;

she warns him of her husband's approach, but too late for he is already upon them. He persuades his wife to spend the night with the boy. Mamma and Marcel go to Marcel's room, and Mamma reads to him from George Sand's *François le Champi:*

> And so, when she read aloud the prose of George Sand, . . . taking pains to banish from her voice any weakness or affectation which might have blocked its channel for that powerful stream of language, she supplied all the natural tenderness, all the lavish sweetness which they demanded to phrases which seemed to have been composed for her voice, and which were all, so to speak, within her compass. She came to them with the tone that they required, with the cordial accent which existed before they were, which dictated them, but which is not to be found in the words themselves, and by these means she smoothed away, as she read on, any harshness there might be or discordance in the tenses of verbs, endowing the imperfect and the preterite with all the sweetness which there is in generosity, all the melancholy which there is in love; guided the sentence that was drawing to an end towards that which was waiting to begin, now hastening, now slackening the pace of the syllables so as to bring them, despite their difference of quantity, into a uniform rhythm, and breathed into this quite ordinary prose a kind of life, continuous and full of feeling.
> My agony was soothed.[11]

With the necessary deletion of "ordinary prose," where is there a better description of the language of Proust and its effects upon the reader than in this description, his own? Starting with this passage, we can see that art for Proust is not merely the discovery of reality, but also the return to the womb. Indeed, it is this return that binds his art with his life and thus functions as his ultimate metaphor, the unfolding of which constitutes his great novel.

Although Proust compares a work of art in which there are theories to an object upon which the price is marked, *A la Recherche du Temps Perdu* is a philosophical novel. In the last volume, the central philosophical ideas of which have already been detailed, Proust does not merely imply or dramatize a theory about reality; he states it. Given the context and the relationship to the whole of the novel, his theory must be understood as an integral part of the novel. *Time Regained* or, at any rate, the latter part does function aesthetically as a culmination of the major philosophical themes as Proust conceives them. He introduces or recapitulates his ideas on involuntary memory, time lost and time regained, essences, intuition, intellect, reality, suffering, happiness, and art. Although he defines only *reality* and fully relates only *art* and *reality*, his use of the other concepts leaves little doubt as to the meaning he attaches or assigns to them.

I shall state the philosophy of *Time Regained* by way of a summary of what has already been said: we live in a world of people, places, and things which are organized spatially or temporally in the everyday, ordinary sense of space and time and which impinge upon us; most of us merely react to the impressions afforded by these phenomena. Even the majority of artists simply responds to rather than penetrates these impressions. The true artist, however, like the scientist, attempts to find the laws that govern these phenomena. The scientist proceeds by his intellect; the artist cannot, for his laws are to be discovered only by intuition. The artist's intellect supplements his intuition, but analysis cannot supplant intuition, that state of mind in which the artist—rooted in past experiences, nourished by suffering, and graced by an involuntary memory of a past sensation joined with a similar present one—extracts the qualitative similarity or essence from these sensations and goes on to embody that essence in a metaphor which, like the essence, is not subject to the laws or ravages of time. Consequently, these essences are the only true reality, and their artistic expression is the only true judgment on reality.

Proust, then, does not deny temporal and spatial relations, nor does he deny the past or the present. But he rejects them as real; hence he must understand by "reality" something quite distinct from "existence." "Reality" for him functions as an honorific term that denotes that which is salvageable from the past, transcends the present, and, therefore, that which is ultimate in the precise sense of being out of time. "Reality" denotes the essences extracted by intuition from what exists in relation to what existed.

That Proust's conceptions of time and intuition are Bergsonian has been and continues to be hotly debated in criticism. Proust, I believe, is not a Bergsonian. Time for Bergson is essentially duration (*durée*); for concepts of the past, the present, and the future cannot apply to the real nature of time because these concepts spatialize time. Duration, which can only be experienced, not thought of or talked about, is the indivisible, ultimate fact of process in the world, and intuition is the experience of duration, a direct acquaintance with it. But for Proust, as we have seen, time is not duration; rather time is the chronological relations of before, now, and after among events. Further, time is not the ultimate reality; only the timeless essences are that; and, finally, intuition is an extraction from, not an immersion in, time.

Nor is Proust a Platonist, as some maintain. To be sure, according to Plato, there are essences which are timeless, but in the sense of perfect forms that have their being independent of the spatial or temporal particulars and qualities of this world. For Plato then, the essences of Proust would be, at most, more or less imperfect copies of the truly real forms.

Proust's conception of essence and intuition is closer perhaps to a Lockean view than it is to either the Bergsonian or Platonic conception. According to Locke's view, there are particulars in the world, among which are sensations or impressions. The mind directly intuits these particulars, their shared qualities, and the universals or similarities that the mind abstracts from them. Now, if we modify this doctrine so that the intuition is sometimes involuntary and encompasses a past as well as a present sensation, not merely two present ones, we have Proust's own view of essence and intuition.

Perhaps Proust has done the exegetical work for us, because the philosophy stated in the last volume explains much of the whole novel: the role of the narrator, especially his attempt to find his vocation as a writer and his preoccupation with literature, music, painting, and architecture; the profusion of metaphors and similes, many of which serve as the expression of Proustian essences, the most famous being the metaphor inspired by the sensation of the madeleine in the cup of tea at Marcel's mother's; the dramatic function of the involuntary memories; many of the characters—as variations on the theme of the "monster-giants" of time; and the persistent search for the laws governing individual and social behavior. But the philosophy of *Time Regained* does not explain or sum up everything: the tremendous range and power of the characterization, the humor, the non-metaphorical prose, the grand metaphors and similes that do not embody essences and are not engendered by involuntary memories or intuitions, the role of the memories that are not involuntary, the penetration of the intellect which operates without the prior aid of intuition, and, most importantly, the philosophical significance and truth of the novel, which are not identical with the dubious ontological-aesthetic claims of *Time Regained*.

The central theme of *A la Recherche du Temps Perdu* is how the novel came to be written. Around this theme the narrator presents and integrates the other themes: childhood, dreams, sleep, love, friendship, society, history, time, knowledge, memory, intuition, art, and reality. The novel consists of many characters, places, events, and things—some borrowed from the actual world, most invented by Proust—and these phenomena are presented as they are observed, analyzed, projected, and remembered by their author. Intuition *is* primary, because it explains genetically why the novel is written and where many of the great metaphors originated. But intuition does not explain how the novel is written—the whole unfolding of and reflection upon character, event, and theme, from Combray to the last Guermantes reception. The emphasis compositionally is on imagination and analysis. Proust creates a world in ordinary chronological time, which world he observes, compares, analyzes, and judges. For this creation to be effective, sharpness and clarity of perception, accuracy in the collection and classification of data, and precision in generalization are essential. Intelligence and insight, not intuition and essence, become the focus of artistic vision.

"In Dostoievski," Marcel remarks to Albertine, "I find the deepest penetration but only into certain isolated regions of the human soul." [12] This incisively brilliant and accurate judgment suggests that Proust's masterpiece similarly embodies a penetration of the deepest kind into at least some of the more accessible regions of the human soul. Proust, I submit, penetrates profoundly those regions of human life that comprise our common emotions, our knowledge of ourselves and others, and our individual and social actions. In effect, he is primarily an individual and social literary psychologist of the human soul. There are none of the Dostoievskian extremes in *A la Recherche du Temps Perdu,* no total commitment to debauchery, buffoonery, criminality, or saintliness. Even the Baron de Charlus is presented as a variant on debauchery, not as its limit. Consequently, if there be any philosophy in Proust's novel that can purport to be true, it is to be found in his understanding of man, not in his theories of art and reality in *Time Regained.*

Illustrating Proust's understanding of man, there is much dramatization of and reflection upon the emotions of jealousy, grief, suffering, and especially love in the novel. At least five major love affairs are depicted: Swann-Odette, Robert de Saint-Loup–Rachel, de Charlus-Morel, Marcel-Gilberte, and Marcel-Albertine. Two of these involve former prostitutes, two involve lesbians, and one involves homosexuals. Only one affair, that of Swann and Odette, ends happily in marriage, but after Swann ceases to love Odette. These relationships are not atypical of love in the novel; they simply highlight most of the other relationships which exist: the Duc and Duchesse de Guermantes, the Verdurins, Robert de Saint-Loup and Gilberte, among them. Only the love-marriage of Marcel's parents stands out as an example of the desirable normal pattern of love and its growth in marriage.

Proust's narration of the major love affairs is justly regarded as one of the achievements of the novel. André Maurois in *The Quest for Proust,* like other critics, extracts a whole philosophy of love from the novel, claiming that this philosophy is new, profound, and tragic, and rivals in its penetration the views of Plato and Schopenhauer.

Maurois points out that the love which Proust conceives and dramatizes is morphological in its nature. It begins in unattached desire and anguish which spur us on to make our choice. Deliberation plays no role in our attachment; every choice springs from a subjective temperament, not from an objective evaluation. In loving a woman, for example, "What we are really doing is to project on her a state of *ourselves*. What matters, therefore, is not the worth of the woman but the profundity of the state. . . ." [13] As a consequence, both the lover and the beloved are involved in a double misconception, in that each expects of the other what each has only imagined to exist. This is why in love "we cannot but choose badly." [14] The discrepancy between the person we have imagined and the person we actually have becomes more and more obvious until the discrepancy gives rise to a basic disillusionment, even in the state of actual possession. But it is here, in disillusionment, that love is aided by other elements in the cycle of love, namely, doubt and consequent jealousy. Even so, love cannot give us what we want. We seek happiness; inevitably we get suffering. Thus, our nature drives us to love with all its attendant illusions; yet the only rewards are continuing misery. Proust, Maurois sums up, is an utter pessimist on love; he destroys it altogether except in its subjective dimension where "the beloved has no real existence outside the imagination of the lover." [15]

If Maurois be correct in his statement of Proust's theory of love, then this theory can be categorized as the formulation of a law about human behavior that is arrived at inductively by observation and intellect and in which intuition, involuntary memory, and ontological metaphor play no role. The metaphors that do appear— like the one in which bits of gossip to Swann about Odette and certain men unknown to Swann are compared to "sentences which dropped into his heart and passed at once into a solid state, grew hard as stalagmites, and seared and tore him as they lay there irremovable" [16]— serve artistically to reinforce the observations. Proust, as artist-philosopher, presents in rich, concrete detail many of the variations on the essence of love.

Now, there can be no denial of the similarities among the love relationships of the novel; the narrator himself frequently points out the similarities, especially as he compares his love for Albertine with Swann's love for Odette. In both Marcel and Swann there is the same need to love, the same initial lack of interest in the woman, the same persistent recognition that the beloved is not a woman in their style, the same inability to break with the woman, the same agitations over lies, the same jealousy that spurs them on, the same disappointment in physical possession, and the same slow process leading to indifference and, in Marcel's case, because of the death of Albertine, to oblivion as well.

Marcel also loves his parents and his grandmother. His parents love each other. Aunt Léonie loved her husband. The Cottards seem happy enough. And those perennial lovers, M. de Norpois and Mme Villeparisis, still adore each other in their declining years. I mention these examples not to sentimentalize love, but to emphasize that any purported theory of the essence of love must accommodate them. And Maurois' interpretation of Proust does not encompass these relationships, nor can any other statement that reduces Proust's depiction of love to an univocal theory. The love shared by Marcel's parents may follow a causal pattern, but it is clearly not one of illusion leading to disillusion. Nor are de Charlus' escapades and desperate affair with Morel essentially like the other affairs; after all, he is broken by his love, not disillusioned.

Proust has no theory of love, no philosophy of its essence, no formulation of a law that covers all cases. His

observant intellect and imagination do not yield a definition of love but a rich harvest of love's ambiguity, vague-
ness, and variety. Proust does not state or even imply the
supposed necessary and sufficient properties—the essence
or nature—of love. Instead he depicts and dramatizes the
multiple range of the criteria of the origin, development,
maturation, disintegration, effects, and value of love.
These criteria include anguish, unattached desire, the influence of environment, lack of deliberation, the subjectivity of choice, projection, the need and sustenance of
suffering, the importance of jealousy, the force of lies,
the role of past loves on a present one, the episodic, dis-
solving character of love, the place of guilt and pity, the
worth of love in its subjective state, the sickness of love,
the devastating role of time in love, the futility of the
search for happiness in love, and the contrary of many of
these.

None of these criteria is a defining property of the love
that Proust portrays. Each is presented, dramatized, en-
larged upon, and interpolated, as it is instanced in some
situation or other. Some of the finest writing in the novel
has to do with the exploration of these criteria. Proust's
analysis of love is philosophical, not because his analysis
ends in a formula, morphological or otherwise, but because it constitutes a dramatization of the conceptual fact
that love has multiple rather than essential criteria. In
effect, Proust does not discover the nature or essence of
love; his search dissolves love's essence into the tantaliz-
ingly inexhaustible experience love is. His artistic vision
—inspired, to be sure, by his intuition, sponsored by his
intellectual and imaginative inductions, and aided by his
microscopic or, as he preferred to call it, telescopic eye—
is leveled on the multiplicities of things, not on their unities. His depiction of the variegations of love manifests
his vision, as do his narrative exfoliations of sleep, dreams,

grief, friendship, self-knowledge, and our knowledge of the external world. It is often said, for example, that Proust denies our knowledge of the external world. The external world exists, but we can never know it. We merely receive impressions from it and project the rest. Proust, consequently, is a subjectivist or perhaps a solipsist, at least epistemologically. Now, it is true that some of the narrator's comments lend support to this interpretation. But here, as in the case of Proust on love, the full text must be kept in mind. For, if the novel embodies such a subjectivist view, what then is to be made of the volumes of social narration? The description of the gathering of the clans, whether the Verdurins' or the Faubourg Saint-Germain's, is ruthless reporting in which individual and collective wit, vulgarity, clichés, foibles, and values are objectively presented and assessed. Further, the composition and history of the late nineteenth-century Parisian *bourgeoisie* and aristocracy, the catalytic impact of the Dreyfus case, and the *mésalliance* of the two classes —castigatingly symbolized by the elevation of the arch-anti-snob, Mme Verdurin, to the arch-snob, the Princesse de Guermantes—are also brilliantly narrated and objectively scrutinized.

Thus, taking the whole novel as evidence, Proust asserts that man can and does have knowledge of the external world, and this includes knowledge of other people: their feelings and motives, their ideals and hypocrisies. Frequently, of course, doubts arise about people, especially those we love. But these doubts are similar to those we entertain about our own feelings and motives. Proust dwells on these uncertainties, but he does not show that resolution is impossible. Marcel, in fact, does resolve his doubt about Albertine and even about himself. So does Swann, after much probing and suffering. Thus, Proust offers no theory of knowledge or its inherent impossibility. What he does with knowledge, especially self-knowledge, is what he does with love: he dramatizes the persistent struggle to clarify and apply the many conflicting and often obscure criteria of our complex feelings and motives. And in this dramatization he rejects rather than affirms essences.

A la Recherche du Temps Perdu is a philosophical novel. Among its themes is the aesthetic-ontological one of the last volume: that ultimate reality is composed of timeless essences which are extracted from things by artistic intuition and transformed into metaphorical equivalents that are exempt from the ravages of time. This theme, although it is genetically basic in the novel as well as majestically conceived and developed, is not a true statement about art and reality. Rather it is Proust's own stipulated redefinition of "art" and "reality."

Another philosophical theme of the novel is the scientific search for the laws governing human behavior, an inquiry that is guided by careful observation and imaginative intelligence. Much of the novel embodies this theme. The narrator seeks the underlying formulas of our common emotional, cognitive, and social life. For those readers or critics of Proust who claim success in this search, the novel is philosophically true because, according to them, it is the dramatization of a number of profound, real definitions of certain controlling features of the human situation, among them, love, grief, suffering, knowledge, and time.

For my own part, I have simply tried to suggest that, although Proust may seek these laws or essences, he does not find them. Instead he discovers that our basic experiences do not have defining properties, that the undeniable, inexhaustible richness and complexity of these experiences preclude such essentialist definitions. To have discovered, explored, and artistically wrought this shatteringly important truth about the unamenability to essentialist definitions of some of our basic human concepts and to have done so a full generation before philosophy itself grasped this conceptual fact are not the least of Proust's achievements in his great novel, itself inexhaustibly rich and complex, defying all attempts at definition.

V. *Epilog*

Candide, Anna Karenina, Hamlet, and *A la Recherche du Temps Perdu,* we have seen, contain as distinguishable although inseparable facets of their artistic unities particular philosophical themes about the nature of man and his world. Philosophical themes inhere in these works just as surely as do characters, dialog, or plot. One important task for literary criticism is to state and clarify these themes, show how they are presented, and relate them to the other aspects of the work. My main concern in these essays has been to attempt this elucidation, for philosophical criticism, as I understand it, is primarily the aesthetic exegesis of the philosophical themes of the literary works that have them. Like an analysis of character, plot, dialog, imagery, or symbolism —when such an analysis elucidates rather than abstracts and isolates—philosophical exegesis is validated as a mode of literary criticism by the fact that it, too, enhances our understanding of the work. Readings of each of the works have been offered, not by interpreting the work in terms of its philosophical theme alone, since this procedure leads to reduction and to distortion, but by interpreting the philosophical theme or themes in relation to the other structural elements—characterization, plot, dialog, and tone. I have defined none of these terms for the very good reason that none of them is definable, at least in the requisite sense of true statements about their corresponding essences. Instead, I have clarified by means of examples these terms, especially "tone," which is neglected in much literary criticism.

What, then, precisely are the philosophical themes of *Candide, Anna Karenina, Hamlet,* and *A la Recherche du Temps Perdu?* How are they presented or dramatized in the particular work? How do they relate to characterization, plot, dialog, tone, and other elements in the particular work?

In *Candide* there are two important philosophical themes: that optimism is absurd and that man does not want utopian happiness. Optimism is the passion for maintaining that all is right when all goes wrong and is tied to the doctrine that our world is rational, benevolent, and teleological and, therefore, that everything is for the best. Utopian happiness is exhibited as an individual and social existence in which the sources of human anxiety are quelled. Voltaire presents the first theme mainly through the plot, an accumulation of horrible experiences that illustrates that ours cannot be the best of all possible worlds; indeed, the evidence points to the probability that ours is the worst. *Candide* dramatizes a caricature of optimism. Unlike a straightforward philosophical assault, it does not attempt to refute the doctrine by argument. In effect, in *Candide,* Voltaire shows that optimism is absurd by dramatizing the absurdity; he does not, as a didactic novelist might, state in dialog or commentary a refutation or *reductio ad absurdum* of optimism. To present the second theme, Voltaire again relies primarily on the plot, but he also, very importantly, comments on the theme through the dialog of some of the characters. Martin's remark that we are born to fluctuate between the

restlessness of anxiety and the lethargy of boredom epito-
mizes the theme that we do not want utopian happiness.

Both themes harmonize with the pervasive tone of the
novel, the romp that is life itself. This tone is aesthetically
basic in *Candide* and functions as the unifying quality of
all the characters, episodes, dialog, and description, with
the exception of the inhabitants of Eldorado who, because
they are neither optimistic nor anxious or bored, are not
human either. Both themes also harmonize with each
other: fraudulent optimism must be repudiated and re-
placed by a true philosophy of life wherein honest labor
is substituted for idle speculation and man must realize
that utopian bliss is not for him, not because he cannot
attain it, but because he does not really want it. He wants
what he has, the romp from anxiety to boredom, which
is life itself.

In *Anna Karenina* there are also two major philosophical themes: that much of human life, if it is creative, not
destructive, is good, and that human transgression of
moral principles is to be punished by God, not by man,
whose duty it is to understand and forgive. Tolstoy states
neither theme in the novel, but both are implicit in the
novel, although the second is but suggested, not stated,
in the epigraph. Having rejected the technique of commentary or interpolation, Tolstoy conveys that creative
human life is good by integrating sympathetic description
with ambivalent narration of Anna's rise and fall. He portrays Anna as a person who rises because she commits herself to the underlying principle of creativity that Tolstoy
so sympathetically describes and who falls because she
violates that principle. Thus, through description and the
character of Anna, Tolstoy illustrates how the very condition of human goodness, creativity, can be obliterated.
The second theme, that it is for God to punish transgression and for man to forgive, is presented primarily

through the plot as it converges on Anna's destruction and through Tolstoy's compassionate treatment of Anna's plight and fall. Anna is shown as justly punished by God, unjustly vilified by those who are morally unfit to judge, and justly forgiven by those who are morally fit to judge.

The two themes merge. We live in a world governed by inexorable moral laws that derive ultimately from God. One of these laws is that nothing in human life can be good without creativity. Consequently, any pursuit of the good that necessitates the rejection of creativity violates the very possibility of the good as well as its natural, and ultimately divine, source. This violation, like any transgression of moral laws, is subject to punishment, but only by God. However, He has decreed more than "Vengeance is mine: I will repay," for it is also written into the universe: "Dearly beloved, avenge not yourselves, but rather give place unto wrath." This whole theme is central in the novel, not, of course, in the sense that everything reduces to it or a variation on it, but in the sense that it aesthetically determines the delineation and range of the characters, the narration of their particular and related lives, the dialog, and the pervasive tone of human largess.

In *Hamlet* many philosophical themes are stated or suggested in the dialog, imagery, characterization, plot, and tone. Among these themes are: that we live in a universe that is teleological and providential, that human life is governed by a "tragic rhythm" from birth to death to regeneration, or that human life is tragic because it inevitably ends in physical corruption, or that the tragic is the spiritual waste that results from the struggle between good and evil in which evil is overcome but good is irretrievably lost, that ours is a moral universe in which we must attain a balance of reason and passion or reason and action in order to avoid divine punishment or an immoral breakdown of the proper relations among our natural attributes, and that ours is a world in which morality is purely subjective or a world about which the basic metaphysical, moral, and epistemological questions, even though they may have answers, are not answered by man.

In spite of the fact that all these themes are present in *Hamlet*, it is an intrusion upon the artistic unity to reduce the play to any one of these themes, for *Hamlet* especially will not yield to such univocal interpretation, philosophical or otherwise, except perhaps to a "second-order" interpretation, according to which no one element—character, plot, dialog, imagery, or tone—is central in the sense that it determines or explains everything else. Every reading of *Hamlet*, from Sir Thomas Hanmer's to those of the present day, fails in its attempt to pluck out the heart of the play and to interpret everything else in terms of it, because such readings leave out certain elements or aspects of the play. In my essay on *Hamlet* I concentrated on this failure in some of the major philosophical univocal readings. But my general conclusion that such readings distort rather than elucidate applies to other univocal readings, psychological, psychoanalytical, and historical, as well. Unlike *Candide* and *Anna Karenina*, or perhaps even *Othello* and *King Lear*, *Hamlet* has no central strand that aesthetically determines and unites the work. It does not follow, however, that *Hamlet* therefore lacks unity, and hence fails as a work of art. For, as Dr. Johnson suggested and Tillyard articulated, the unity of *Hamlet* consists in its explication of the great variety of human experience in its cosmic setting.

The complexity of *Hamlet* does more than to call into question univocal readings. It also mirrors the major philosophical theme in the play: that our world is irreducibly complex. Thus the critics of *Hamlet* who attempt to reduce its complexity to a central strand are like the philosophers who try to reduce to a basic principle the complexity of the world that *Hamlet* mirrors. Both attempts fail because these two worlds that reflect each other yield no single or pervasive formula. Hamlet's admonition to Guildenstern defies us all. That we live in a world which is irreducibly complex, hence that basic metaphysical, moral, and epistemological questions can be asked but not answered, is the philosophical theme in *Hamlet* that integrates best with the other strands. For one thing, it explains the presence and function of the other philosophical themes in *Hamlet* that have played such havoc with traditional philosophical criticism of the play. These themes in their dramatic contexts are not affirmations; they are queries about the nature of man and his cosmic setting. Hamlet, for example, does not state the nature of man; he asks whether the traditional conception is true. Human and cosmic complexities engender basic doubts; neither the complexities nor the doubts are resolved in the play. But they are translated into Hamlet's delay and inaction, his meditations, probings, imaginative flights, and even his tragedy which Horatio, like Bradley, regards with wonder. Hamlet's notorious irresolution is not so much a symptom of infirmity as it is a manifestation of his intellectual integrity that cannot rest content with the traditional philosophical answers and yet cannot pluck a new answer out of the universe. The philosophical theme of the irreducible complexity of the world is important in *Hamlet*. But it is not central in it—nothing is; like the characters, dialog, plot, imagery, symbolism, and tone, it functions as one contributing element in the irreducible artistic complex that is *Hamlet*.

A la Recherche du Temps Perdu Proust avows to be a

philosophical novel. From the first volume, *Swann's Way*, to the last, *Time Regained*, the narrator, Marcel, perseveres in his search for "a philosophic theme for some great literary work" until, at the very moment when he thinks he has repudiated forever his search, he finally discovers that reality is composed of timeless essences which are extracted from the world by artistic intuition and transformed into their symbolic equivalents, works of art which, like the essences, are beyond the ravages of time. Also implicit in this theme are conceptions concerning time, physical objects, sense-knowledge, memory, and intellect, as these relate to or contrast with art and reality. The traditional dichotomy between appearance and reality is not stressed; rather the distinction between what is real, in time, and what is *ultimately* real, out of time, is considered.

The essences that purportedly constitute ultimate reality and the subject matter of art depend for their existence on the sense-impressions derived from a spatially and temporally related world of persons, objects, and places, since a necessary condition for their emergence is the past and its salvageability and the present and the transcendence of it through involuntary memory and intuition. Time cannot be regained if it never exists.

Most of us merely react to these impressions, never even attempting to penetrate them. The (true) artist, however, makes this effort in his struggle to discover the analogies of the scientific laws that govern these phenomena. Unlike the scientist who employs intellect in his search, the artist must proceed primarily with his intuition, using his intellect only as a supplement. Intuition is the mental act in which the artist penetrates his range of sense-phenomena through an extraction of the qualitative similarity between two sensations, a present one joined with a past one, and embodies that similarity, which is the essence, in a metaphor which, like the essence, is outside of time. This act of intuition depends upon certain conditions without which it does not occur: past experiences, suffering, and involuntary memory. When these conditions are present, the realm of sense-phenomena is penetrated; the essences abstracted from these phenomena, as enchained in the language of metaphor, become the work of art and through it become a true judgment on the nature of ultimate reality. This theme is presented primarily by direct statement and detailed exposition by the narrator, who is both participant and observer, especially in the last volume, *Time Regained*. But Proust employs more than the traditional novelist's technique of interpolation in his presentation; he also suggests various aspects of the theme throughout the novel in the characterization, dialog, and plot. Therefore, when the theme is rendered fully explicit in the final volume, the direct statement of it serves aesthetically as climax and culmination. The search for essences and their metaphorical equivalents, the struggle to penetrate the meaning of appearances, the growing, painful awareness of the destructive character of time, the periodic visitations of involuntary memory, the persistent fascination for the monster-giants as well as the monstrous dwarfs in time, the over-all preoccupation with art as a vocation, suggested and implied, emerge as themes long before the epiphany at the Prince de Guermantes'. Even the existence, creation, and structure of the novel embody the theme, for the novel represents the great victory of indestructible art over the ravages of time.

However, this theme does not explain the range and power of the characterization, the humor, the nonmetaphorical prose, the metaphors that are not expressions of essences or are not caused by involuntary memory, the role of voluntary memory, the importance of the intellect which functions independent of prior intuition, and the philosophical theme of the dissolution of essences in the very search for them. Indeed, integrated in the novel is a nether theme according to which our basic emotions and cognitive states have no essences, no sets of necessary and sufficient properties, and from which it follows that there are no corresponding real, true definitions or theories of these experiences. The search for the essences or laws that govern these experiences uncovers multiplicities, not unities; these multiplicities foreclose upon the very possibility of traditional essentialist definitions. Intellect supplants, it does not supplement, intuition. Observation, analysis, and generalization dissolve the perennial search for definitions of our basic emotional and cognitive experiences into the shocking discovery that the criteria of these experiences are multiple rather than essential. Although Proust never states this theme of the indefinability of basic emotional and cognitive experiences and their corresponding concepts, he does exhibit the multiple range of the criteria of basic emotional and cognitive concepts, especially by a dramatization of the persistent, painful struggle on the part of human beings to clarify and apply the many conflicting and often obscure criteria of their complex feelings and motives. Proust's treatment of love is the best example of the dissolution of essences in the search for them. His probing exhibition of love's great variety reveals an inexhaustible set of properties, no one of which is necessary, no collection of which is sufficient. Rather than a dramatization of a particular definition of love, Proust dramatizes, through the relations of the narrator and Gilberte, the narrator and Albertine, Swann and Odette, de Charlus and Morel, Robert de Saint-Loup and Rachel, the Duc and Duchesse de Guermantes, the Verdurins, Marcel's parents, Marcel and his grandmother, M. de Norpois and Mme Villeparisis, and others, that love is too ambiguous, vague, and varied to be encompassed by any essentialist definition.

This theme of the dissolution of essence relates also to the characterization, dialog, plot, tone, and commentary. There is much searching in the novel. Not all of this searching is for the essences of intuition and art. Some converges on attempts to clarify, hence to have certain knowledge of, particular feelings and motives. These attempts, whether directed toward oneself or others, involve much probing and suffering. Individual characters sometimes know how they feel or how others feel toward them. But for the most part they do not, and because they do not, they are desperate. The hell of their uncertainty is the emotional counterpart of the philosophical truth they are forced to learn and to live with, that they cannot resolve their terrible uncertainties by an appeal to essences, to true definitions that make everything clear, because the appeal increases rather than resolves the doubts. We can explain in no other way the hundreds of pages that Proust devotes to the meticulous quest for certainty, especially Swann's and later the narrator's. Their certainty comes only when they know they no longer love their mistresses; they do not resolve their doubts about whether they love until it is determined that they no longer love. Thus, Proust dramatizes the uncertainty that has to do with the application of the many conflicting and obscure criteria of an emotion, not the uncertainty about whether a clear definition of an emotion applies.

The two philosophical themes that reality consists of timeless essences which only art can discover and that our concepts of emotions and motives are unamenable to essentialist definitions also integrate. The first explains the genesis, as well as the last judgment of the novel, and the structure of the work. The second explains a good deal of the characterization, plot, and especially the persistent tone of the search for a certainty about our emotional and cognitive life, which certainty comes only when it is too late for us to assuage the painful doubts. The second theme is absorbed by the first—art assimilates life, but only at the end of the novel. The rest of the novel constitutes the epitome of an art that is inspired by an intellect which is autonomous. The Proustian vision remains in time.

Philosophical exegesis of our four examples, if we may generalize from them, reveals that at least some works of literature contain philosophical themes, that themes can be presented explicitly through dialog and commentary or implicitly through characterization, plot, dialog, description, or tone, that themes relate and contribute aesthetically to the other structural elements as well as to the unity of the whole work, and that, while a particular theme may be either central or simply one among many contributing elements, the work cannot be reduced to the theme or a series of variations on it without violating the artistic integrity of the work. However, it would exaggerate the role of philosophy in literature to contend that every poem, play, or novel has a philosophical theme, for there are lyrics that are pure expressions of feeling, plays that are simple fantasy or exciting melodrama, and novels that are sheer entertainment. Among fine literary works there are those whose artistic value is quite independent of any philosophical theme. Of course it is possible, indeed for some critics necessary, to impose philosophy upon every literary work, and some philosophers even project philosophy on all works of art. But such wholesale philosophical exegesis does aesthetic injustice to those works of art which omit explicit or implicit philosophical themes.

Critics and aestheticians often ask whether philosophical themes in literature are statements or truth-claims about the world. Of central importance in answering this question is to realize that the question is not the factual one it purports or seems to be. It is rather the normative question, should philosophical themes in literature be read as statements or truth-claims about the world? The question is normative, not factual, because, although philosophical themes are present in (at least some) literature in the way that characters and plot are, whether or not these themes are to be regarded as statements or truth-claims about the world depends upon the reader's inclination and not on the themes' actually being statements or truth-claims. Themes are no more statements or truth-claims about the world than narrations of characters, events, or places in literature are descriptions of actual persons, events, or places. Aestheticians like Croce and literary critics like Richards, who wish their literature neat, unmixed with the muddy waters of the world, argue that to avoid distorting literature we ought not to read themes as statements or truth-claims. But this is not cogent, for although we distort literature when we insist that everything in literature is about the world, we do not distort literature when we ask whether its themes refer to the real world. Hence, I see no good reason to reject or even to debate any longer the traditional, conventional interpretation of the printed or implied philosophical themes in literature as statements or truth-claims about the world. To persevere in this interpretation, as I have shown in my particular exegeses, is to enrich, not to distort, literature.

We must ask next whether these themes, if read as statements or truth-claims about the world, are actually true and verifiable? Let us return to our four examples. In *Candide* that optimism is absurd and that man wants the romp between boredom and anxiety rather than utopian bliss are themes more easily established as verifiable than as true. The evidence that ours is not the best of all possible worlds and that man loves the romp of life is ample but not sufficient to establish the truth about our world or man's fundamental desire in it. As the evidence stands, Voltaire's claims remain artistic insights, not verified truths. The theme in *Anna Karenina* that we live in a world of divine, inexorable laws is unverifiable, except perhaps in the naturalistic paraphrase of one aspect of the theme, that we must create in order to achieve human value. But even in this paraphrase, it is extremely difficult to render the claim sufficiently precise to determine just what would count as evidence for or against it. Of course, the whole theme may be true; but until we are more sure about God and His universe than we are or are likely to be, the theme remains a matter of mere speculation. In *Hamlet*, that we live in a world which is irreducibly complex, hence that the basic metaphysical, moral, and epistemological questions about it can be asked but not answered, is also verifiable and, so far as one can tell, true. The two themes in *A la Recherche du Temps Perdu*—that reality consists of timeless essences which only art can discover and that our concepts of emotions and motives are unamenable to essentialist definitions because their corresponding experiences have no essences—must be separated. The first is neither verifiable nor true; it is stipulation, pure and simple. The second is verifiable and true, a profound philosophical claim about the relation between language and the world.

For many readers the truth of these philosophical themes enhances and their falsity detracts from the aesthetic value of the literary works that contain them. It is simply a fact that true themes, for example, function as one criterion of merit in aesthetic judgments of literature.

However, in recent aesthetics and literary criticism, this criterion has been challenged on the grounds that it is neither necessary, sufficient, nor relevant to aesthetic merit. I agree with the recent view that this criterion is not sufficient because, if it were, literature (and art) would reduce to philosophy; and that it is not necessary because, if it were, literary works that contain false themes could not be good or great literature. The first consequence destroys literature; the second contradicts one of the basic beliefs of the well-wrought reader, namely, that much of the world's great literature contains false themes about the world. That the truth of themes is neither necessary nor sufficient for aesthetic value in literature, however, is not a matter of fact, but of principle, that one can accept or reject. The principle, moreover, cannot be justified as self-evident; its sole justification is its consequences, the main one being that it enables us to respond favorably to much acknowledged great literature which philosophically is false. Unless we accept this principle that the truth of themes is neither necessary nor sufficient for aesthetic value in literature, we must forsake all those literary masterpieces whose philosophical themes are false or regarded by us as false. For most of us, to dismiss this principle is to foreclose upon almost all of the world's great literature.

However, although the truth of a theme is not necessary or sufficient for the aesthetic merit of a literary work, it is relevant. The truth of any of the themes in our four literary works enhances the aesthetic value of the particular work of which it is an integral part. It adds another dimension to the work, contributing to it not merely as a philosophical theme on an aesthetic par with the characters and plot, but as a true theme, or one taken by the reader to be true. The insights of *Candide*, which I consider to be true although I cannot produce enough evidence to establish their truth, increase the value of that work. The theme in *Hamlet,* because it fuses with the characterization, dialog, plot, and tone, and also because it is true (at any rate, for me), contributes to the greatness of the play. The nether theme in *A la Recherche du Temps Perdu,* in its sheer dimension of a true as well as an original philosophical claim about the role of basic concepts of and in experience, adds to the total magnificence of the work of art; and it does so because it is dramatized effectively and is integrated fully with the characterization, plot, and especially tone. Thus, a necessary condition for the aesthetic enhancement by a true theme of any literary work is that the truth as well as the theme contribute artistically to the work. If this condition is satisfied, as it is in three of our examples, I see no good reason for rejecting the relevance of the truth of the theme to the aesthetic value of the work. True themes, I submit, are as relevant to the artistic merit of literary works as are convincing characterization and probable plots.

So far as false themes or themes believed to be false are concerned, they are neither necessary nor sufficient for artistic demerit of the literary works that possess them because, if they were, then every literary work with a false theme would be deficient. But there are faulty literary works that have no such themes, and literary works with false themes which are not failures, but masterpieces. *Anna Karenina* is one of them. What, now, of the relevance of false themes to the aesthetic value of the literary works containing them? Should, for example, the falsity of the theological-moral theme of *Anna Karenina* or of the aesthetic-ontological theme of *A la Recherche du Temps Perdu* (or at any rate, the belief that they are false) detract from the aesthetic value of these works? The dictates of a uniform view require that if true themes are aesthetically relevant, so are false ones. But the requirement can and should be relinquished for one that enables us to accommodate literary works, especially great ones, whose philosophical themes are false. This requirement is that we waive the false theme, hence its relevance to artistic merit, and interpret it instead as a way of looking at the world. Our philosophical exegesis thus shifts from how the false theme functions in the work to how the theme, as an imaginative possibility for the world, becomes an integral part of the world created by the writer. That ours is a divinely ordained, moral universe or that reality is a realm of timeless essences to be grasped only by artistic intuition is false or, at any rate, regarded as false by many. Nevertheless, like Fate in the Greek tragedies, Purgatory and Paradise in *The Divine Comedy*, or The Still Point of the Turning World in the *Four Quartets*, they constitute exciting possibilities in our thinking about the world. We would not be wiser without them, for they help build imaginative pictures of how things should or might be, which serve as perpetual challenges to our scientific and philosophical efforts to state exactly how things are.

This last consideration brings us to our final problem of the difference between philosophical themes in literature and philosophy proper, where by "philosophy proper" I do not mean what philosophy should be, but what it is, including what philosophers have thought it ought to be from Thales to Wittgenstein. The philosophy of our age is especially self-conscious about its nature, aims, and purposes; it would be an historical error, however, to infer from this that present philosophy is unique in this respect, for philosophers perennially debate not only particular philosophical doctrines about reality, truth, knowledge, morality, and value, but also philosophy itself. Nevertheless, in spite of the great disagreements over doctrine as well as over method and aim, there are certain areas of agreement. Two important ones are the quest for true doctrines about the nature of reality, knowledge, morality, value, and philosophy itself, and the insistence upon argument to support these doctrines, where the argument turns on logical or empirical procedures and truths. To discover true statements about how things are or ought to be is the aim of philosophy, even if philosophy is conceived of, as it is by many today, as the elucidation of the logical or "grammatical" features of language. But to provide these true statements is not enough for philosophy; these statements must also be supported by evidence, conceptual or empirical, which serves in the argument for the statements. Indeed, the argument, that is, the collecting and ordering of the conceptual and empirical evidence, because it requires great skill, imagination, subtlety, clarity, and often genius, is more important in any particular philosophical view than the mere statement of true doctrines.

Philosophical themes in literature similarly function as statements or truth-claims about how things are or how they ought to be. So the difference between philosophy in literature and philosophy proper cannot be in their aims, which are alike. They differ, then, primarily in their mode of presentation in that philosophy in literature supplants argument by dramatization. The philosophical theme, whether stated or implied in dialog, description, tone, or commentary, is shown, not argued for except incidentally as, for example, in *Candide* where the arguments for optimism are parodied while the *reductio* of optimism is given in the story, or in *Time Regained* where arguments are offered for an aesthetic-ontological doctrine, yet serve artistically mainly to articulate what has already been dramatized in the whole of *A la Recherche du Temps Perdu*. But to show the theme in literature is not to prove or confirm it. The terms that are applicable to philosophical arguments—proof, demonstration, support, and confirmation—are inappropriate to the themes of literature. Voltaire, Tolstoy, Shakespeare, and Proust, in the works we have examined, exhibit certain philosophical themes. These authors emphasize the richness of illustrative detail, not the economy of cogent argument. Coherence, concreteness, and integration are appropriate terms for their presentations of philosophy. Are the themes intelligible, whether they are true or not, verifiable or not? Are they displayed in depictions of human beings, their lives, and their interrelations? Do they relate and contribute to the characterization, dialog, plot, description, and tone of the particular work of literature? These are among the aesthetically legitimate questions we can ask of philosophical themes in literature. When we provide convincing affirmative answers to these questions, as we can in regard to our four examples and which I have tried to do, our exegetical assignment is completed, for we have shown that philosophy can be applied to literature and, by implication, that literature can contain philosophy. Philosophy can be combined with literature, then, to their mutual enrichment and not, as many hold, to their mutual distortion and denigration. Indeed, philosophy proper has much to learn from philosophy in literature: about philosophy and not merely about literature. When the themes are false, or believed to be false, they nonetheless serve in their rich, concrete applications as radical possibilities in our philosophical thinking about the world. *Anna Karenina*, like the Greek tragedies, enables us to grasp in great detail the meaning and import of a world whose basic structure is moral and divine. Also when the themes are true, or believed to be true, they serve as radical reminders in our philosophical thinking about the world. *Candide, Hamlet,* and *A la*

Recherche du Temps Perdu are supreme in this regard; the first, because it forces us to question any purported panacea for the ills of mankind; and the other two, because their dramatization of the fundamental irreducibility of the world to a formula acts as a necessary admonition to philosophy itself to tread lightly on the glorious complexity of the world if it wishes to see it in flower.

Notes

Candide

1. Voltaire, *Candide*, trans. John Butt (Harmondsworth, 1947), p. 96.
2. *Ibid.*, p. 86.
3. Voltaire, *Candide*, ed. Lester G. Crocker (London, 1958), p. 70.
4. Butt, p. 144.
5. *Ibid.*, p. 143.
6. *Ibid.*, p. 144.
7. Crocker, p. 106.
8. Butt, p. 82.
9. Crocker, p. 68.
10. Butt, pp. 82-83.
11. *Candide*, ed. Norman L. Torrey (New York, 1946), p. 59.
12. Butt, p. 57.
13. *Ibid.*, p. 140.
14. *Loc. cit.*
15. Crocker, p. 104.

Anna Karenina

1. Leo Tolstoy, *Anna Karenina*, trans. Constance Garnett (New York, 1950), pp. 91-92.
2. *Ibid.*, p. 194.
3. *Ibid.*, p. 299.
4. *Ibid.*, p. 158.
5. *Ibid.*, pp. 176-177.

6. *Ibid.*, p. 346.
7. *Ibid.*, p. 168.
8. *Ibid.*, p. 226.
9. *Ibid.*, p. 712.
10. *Ibid.*, p. 816.
11. *Ibid.*, p. 4.
12. *Ibid.*, p. 51.
13. *Ibid.*, p. 101.
14. *Ibid.*, p. 122.
15. *Ibid.*, p. 378.
16. *Ibid.*, p. 744.
17. *Ibid.*, p. 749.
18. *Ibid.*, p. 817.
19. *Ibid.*, p. 905.
20. *Ibid.*, p. 84.
21. *Ibid.*, p. 489.

Hamlet

1. T. S. Eliot, "Hamlet," *Selected Essays* (London, 1932), p. 141.

2. All quotations from *Hamlet* are from *The New Shakespeare*, ed. John Dover Wilson (Cambridge, 1934). Hereafter, references to this work will appear in the text following the quoted material.

3. Lily B. Campbell, *Shakespeare's Tragic Heroes: Slaves of Passion* (New York, 1952), p. 38.

4. *Ibid.*, p. 109.

5. *Ibid.*, p. 132.

6. *Ibid.*, p. 147.

7. Caroline F. E. Spurgeon, *Shakespeare's Imagery and What It Tells Us* (Boston, 1958), p. 9.

8. *Ibid.*, p. 316.

9. *Ibid.*, pp. 318-319 (italics in original).

10. Wolfgang H. Clemen, *The Development of Shakespeare's Imagery* (London, 1951), p. 113.

11. *Ibid.*, p. 111.

12. *Ibid.*, p. 112.

13. *Loc. cit.*

14. Francis Fergusson, *The Idea of a Theater* (Princeton, 1949), p. 120.

15. *Loc. cit.*
16. *Ibid.*, p. 122.
17. *Ibid.*, pp. 127-128.
18. *Ibid.*, p. 139.
19. *Ibid.*, p. 127.
20. E. E. Stoll, *Hamlet: A Historical and Comparative Study* ("Research Publications of the University of Minnesota," VIII, No. 5 [1919]), 63.
21. John Dover Wilson, *The New Shakespeare, Hamlet* (Cambridge, 1934), pp. lx-lxi.
22. Samuel T. Coleridge, *Shakespearean Criticism*, ed. Thomas M. Raysor (2 vols.; London, 1960), I, 16.
23. *Ibid.*, II, 230.
24. *Ibid.*, I, 18 (italics in original).
25. *Ibid.*, II, 150.
26. *Loc. cit.*
27. *Ibid.*, I, 34.
28. *Ibid.*, p. 35.
29. *Ibid.*, II, 154-155.
30. John Dover Wilson, *What Happens in 'Hamlet'* (Cambridge, 1935), p. 229.
31. A. C. Bradley, *Shakespearean Tragedy* (New York, 1955), p. 40.
32. E. M. W. Tillyard, *Shakespeare's Problem Plays* (London, 1957), p. 17.
33. *Ibid.*, pp. 26-27.
34. *Ibid.*, p. 28.
35. *Ibid.*, p. 31.

A la Recherche du Temps Perdu

1. Marcel Proust, *Remembrance of Things Past*, trans. C. K. Scott Moncrieff and Stephen Hudson (12 vols.; London, 1941), XII, 200.
2. *Ibid.*, pp. 209-210.
3. *Ibid.*, p. 216.
4. *Ibid.*, p. 239.
5. *Ibid.*, p. 248; p. 262.
6. *Ibid.*, p. 248.
7. *Ibid.*, p. 293.
8. *Ibid.*, pp. 433-434.

9. *Ibid.*, 1, 246.

10. *Ibid.*, p. 250.

11. *Ibid.*, p. 55.

12. *Ibid.*, X, 239-240.

13. Proust, *op. cit.*, IV, 184, as quoted by André Maurois, *The Quest for Proust*, trans. Gerald Hopkins (London, 1950), p. 214.

14. Quoted by Maurois, *op. cit.*, p. 215.

15. Maurois, *ibid.*, p. 237.

16. Proust, *op. cit.*, II, 137.

Index

Index

Johnson, Samuel, 11, 65, 95
Jones, Ernest, 62

King Lear, 64, 95
Kyd, Thomas, 57

Leibniz, Gottfried Wilhelm, 15
Levin, Harry, 66
Literary terms: definition of, 9,
    91-92
Literature: and philosophy, 7, 9,
    91-109 *passim;* and truth, 102-
    06; as emotive, 8; definition of,
    9, 91-92; elements of, 9
Locke, John, 80

Maurois, André: on Proust's the-
    ory of love, 82-84
Myth and ritual, 54-55

Odyssey, 54
Oedipus Rex: compared to *Ham-
    let*, 54, 56
Olivier, Sir Laurence, 44
Othello, 64, 95

Philosophical themes: and truth-
    claims, 92-101; relevance to lit-
    erary merit, 101-06
Philosophy: and criticism, 101; as
    exegetical tool, 10-11; how pre-
    sented in literature, 92; opposed
    to literature, 7; "proper," 106-
    07
Plato, 7, 8, 15, 18, 79-80
Pope, Alexander, 15
"Problem play," 64

Proust, Marcel, 26, 71-88 *passim*,
    96, 98, 99, 100, 101, 108. *See also
    A la Recherche du Temps
    Perdu*

Richards, I. A.: aesthetics of lit-
    erature, 8; rejection of philos-
    ophy in literature, 8; men-
    tioned, 7, 11, 102

St. Paul, 36
Sand, George, 77
Schopenhauer, Arthur, 82
Seneca, 57
Shakespeare, William, 43-67 *pas-
    sim*, 108. *See also Hamlet*
Spencer, Theodore, 46
Spurgeon, Caroline F.: as imagis-
    tic critic, 10; on *Hamlet*, 50-52;
    mentioned, 56
Stoll, E. E., 56-58

Thales, 106
Tillyard, E. M. W., 63-65, 95
Tolstoy, Leo, 25-39 *passim*, 93, 94,
    108. *See also Anna Karenina*
Tragedy: possibility of definition
    of, 63
Truth-claims, 102-06

Voltaire, 7-21 *passim*, 92, 103, 108.
    See also Candide

Wilson, John Dover: on *Hamlet*,
    62; on Stoll, 58-59
Wittgenstein, L., 9, 106

116

The manuscript was edited by Patricia Davis. The book was designed by Richard Kinney. The type face is Linotype Janson cut by Mergenthaler Linotype in 1932. Janson is based on the type face cut by Nicholas Kis in Amsterdam, 1690, but erroneously accredited to Anton Janson. The display face is Caslon #540 based on the original design of William Caslon, 1725.

The book is printed on Warren's 1854 Text. The soft cover edition is bound in Warren's Lustro Gloss Cover and the hard cover edition is bound in Joanna Mills Natullin cloth. Manufactured in the United States of America.